D.I.V.A.
DIARIES

BLACK STUDIES
& critical thinking

Rochelle Brock and Richard Greggory Johnson III
Executive Editors

Vol. 58

The Black Studies and Critical Thinking series
is part of the Peter Lang Education list.
Every volume is peer reviewed and meets
the highest quality standards for content and production.

PETER LANG
New York • Bern • Frankfurt • Berlin
Brussels • Vienna • Oxford • Warsaw

DIARIES

The Road to the Ph.D.
and Stories of Black Women
Who Have Endured

Edited by
Cherrel Miller Dyce
and Toni Milton Williams

PETER LANG
New York • Bern • Frankfurt • Berlin
Brussels • Vienna • Oxford • Warsaw

Library of Congress Cataloging-in-Publication Data

D.I.V.A. diaries: the road to the Ph.D. and stories of black women
who have endured / edited by Cherrel Miller Dyce, Toni Milton Williams.
Pages cm. — (Black studies and critical thinking; Vol. 58)
Includes bibliographical references.
1. African American women scholars—Biography. 2. Doctoral students—
United States—Biography. 3. Doctoral students—United States—Social conditions.
4. Doctor of philosophy degree—United States. I. Dyce, Cherrel Miller,
editor of compilation, author. II. Williams, Toni Milton, editor of compilation,
author. III. Title: DIVA diaries.
LC2781.D46   378.1'982996073—dc23   2014048952
ISBN 978-1-4331-2385-6 (hardcover)
ISBN 978-1-4331-2384-9 (paperback)
ISBN 978-1-4539-1521-9 (e-book)
ISSN 1947-5985

Bibliographic information published by **Die Deutsche Nationalbibliothek**.
Die Deutsche Nationalbibliothek lists this publication in the "Deutsche
Nationalbibliografie"; detailed bibliographic data are available
on the Internet at http://dnb.d-nb.de/.

We dedicate this book to all DIVAS whose work is represented through our collective voices. The wall of Black women is a constant reminder of our common struggles and victories. To those Black women who will come after us, we say, for unto whomsoever much is given, of him shall be much required. Solidarity!

Cherrel dedicates this book to her mother, Ilene, and to her late grandmother, fondly known in their small Jamaican community as Ms. Dasa, may her soul rest in peace. She carries both of your fighting spirits, love, and passion for the community in the deepest areas of her soul. She also dedicates this book to her husband Mark and their three children.

Toni dedicates this book to her parents Beatrice T. Milton and the late Jimmie L. Milton Sr. for their infinite love and wisdom. She also dedicates the book to her husband Mike and their two rugrats and the rest of her family for their unwavering support.

Contents

Acknowledgments

We would first like to acknowledge the women in our families who have gone before us and paved the way. If not for your wisdom, persistence, support, passion, and love we would not be the women we are today.

We would like to thank all those who have supported DIVAS and our mission. Special thanks to Dr. Jean Rohr, for planting the seed for this narrative.

Introduction: Inception of the Distinguished, Intellectual, Virtuous, Academic Sistas (DIVAS) Collective

CHERREL MILLER DYCE, TONI MILTON WILLIAMS,
AND TORRY REYNOLDS

The Courage
By Cherrel Miller Dyce

The beating of my heart reached a rhythm that produced an unsteady gait
My eyes became enlarged as I search the openness for your presence
Unconsciously we connect in shared silence with our pain as our thread
How could this be, this should have never happened, overflowing sorrow
Gather ourselves to a place in the spirit; gather ourselves to the plains of tomorrow
Victory is upon the horizon, the sun leading us onward to glory
Not now, not ever will we succumb
Never will we relinquish our grace, hopes, our joys, our heritage
Call yonder for our courage, as we press onwards for the sisters of tomorrow.

There is myriad research recently conducted about the success of Black women who are completing graduate programs. According to Holmes, Land, and Hinton-Hudson (2007), "the journey to higher education for many Black women has been long and arduous" (p. 106). The extant research literature is saturated with studies discussing doctoral student experiences. Studies have highlighted the role of social and cultural expectation (Golde, 2000), marginality (Gay, 2004), and identity development (Gardner, 2009). While African Americans only account for 14% of those enrolled in post-baccalaureate study, 65% of all doctoral degrees conferred to African Americans are earned by Black women (Aud et al., 2012). These studies are foundational because they intersect the current crises in doctoral education. According to the Council of Graduate Schools (2012):

Increasing demand for workers with advanced training at the graduate level, an inadequate domestic talent pool, and a small representation of women and minority graduates at all education levels are among some growing concerns over workforce issues that relate to the vitality and competitiveness of the U.S. economy. Improving completion rates for all doctoral students, and particularly for those from underrepresented groups, is vital to meeting our nation's present and future workforce needs. (para. 1)

For Black women in academe, the issue of persistence and completion is compounded by factors such as race and racism (Patton, 2004), self-efficacy and marginality (Hinton, 2010), and socialization and gender (Ellis, 2001). From its inception, DIVAS (Distinguished, Intellectual, Virtuous, Academic Sistas) has allowed Black women doctoral students and new professionals to "stand in the gap" and become the "othermother" (Case, 1997; Foster, 1993; Guiffrida, 2005) as well as become fictive kin (Cook, 2010; Ebaugh & Curry 2000; Fordham, 1996) for Black women during their PhD process and into the academy.

In an early study of African American women scholars at predominately White institutions conducted by Moses (1989), among the problems typical of African American women faculty and administrators were lack of professional support and denial of access to power structures normally associated with their positions. Given these realities, *DIVA Diaries* presents the collective experiences of Black women doctoral students and emerging professionals as we navigated intersecting identities as not only Black women but also as wives, mothers, daughters, teachers, students, and novice researchers. DIVAS was formed in 2009 as a collective to address the unique concerns, hidden rules, and perspectives of Black female PhD students attending a public predominately White institution in the southeastern United States. After being told by DIVA Cherrel at our first meeting that "we are the Black face of education for tomorrow," we immediately established a critical community and decided to continue meeting to support one another. According to Bettez (2011), fostering critical community among graduate students can help alleviate negative feelings and difficulties brought on by graduate studies. As institutions of higher education are grappling with the high percentage of students not completing the PhD, the DIVAS collective and our book *DIVA Diaries* provides stories from Black women of triumph through resilience, courage, community, and faith. We introduce the term "Black-centric critical consciousness" to name this collective experience. Furthermore, it provides awareness for Black women of their retention and needs while undertaking the PhD process.

A DIVACentric Epistemology: Conceptual Foundation

Othermothering

Conceptual foundations of DIVAS are twofold. The primary concept upon which DIVAS is built is othermothering. The practice of othermothering is a long-standing tradition in the African American community (Case, 1997; Guiffrida, 2005). Through othermothering, extended family and community members would come alongside a child to supplement the childrearing efforts of the biological mother (Guiffrida, 2005). When applied to the academy, othermothering becomes a means through which students are mentored, advised, challenged, and supported throughout their educational journey by others who have advanced standing in the institution. The DIVAS embrace this practice and incorporate it in to each of our activities. We are a sisterhood of Black women who value our shared history and understand the threads of ancestry that have othermothered, and now othersistered us. In highlighting our common African-centered lineage, Collins (1989) asserts that:

> Moreover, as a result of colonialism, imperialism, slavery, apartheid, and other systems of racial domination, Blacks share a common experience of oppression. These similarities in material conditions have fostered shared Afrocentric values that permeate the family structure, religious institutions, culture, and community life of Blacks in varying parts of Africa, the Caribbean, South America, and North America. This Afrocentric consciousness permeates the shared history of people of African descent through the framework of a distinctive Afrocentric epistemology. (Collins, 1989, p. 755)

Since Patricia Hill Collins's introduction of the concept (Bernard et al., 2000), othermothering has been used as a framework for understanding the sociocultural, political, and historical experiences of Black women in the academy. As a catalyst for meaning-making, the concept of othermothering is socially constructed (Bryant, 1999) and is represented in myriad ways in the research literature. Bryant (1999) used the term "manymothering" to represent the psychological nature of the term. Manymothering is defined as "the many, actual, contemporary, and historic women who have provided mothering functions to their African American daughters" (p. 2). Essentially, Bryant's work centered on psychoanalytic thought as it relates to the experiences of Black women by underscoring the role of race, culture, class, history, and oppression on how Black women psychologically interact with family, self, community, and the wider social institutions (1999). In the DIVAS collective, "this idea of othermothers differs from a Western-European perspective that embraces exclusive mothering versus kinship mothering" (Bryant, 1999,

p. 1), thus allowing for hybridity in using the concept. Manymothering, like othermothering, is not dependent on blood ties and this allows for hybridity in the othermothering concept as the social networks in the DIVAS embraces fictive and non-fictive kin relationships in order to combat isolation and marginality in the academy.

Likewise, Bernard et al.'s (2000) research provides validity for the international application of the othermothering concept. These researchers used the concept to make visible the experiences of African Canadian and African Caribbean students and faculty in Canada as it relates to academic marginality, feminist discourse, and gender inequality. In this qualitative study, the voices of students and faculty highlighted issues such as isolation, self-concept, and mentoring. A central reflection in this study is the concept that "She who learns teaches" (p. 82). Teaching others within the social network of the DIVAS is expected, as those who are more senior DIVAS are expected to teach in both formal and informal ways in order to increase the academic and social success of each member.

More recent studies (Griffin, 2013; Mawhinney, 2012) using othermothering as a narrative for understanding the academic spaces of Black students and faculty have been complimentary to Bernard et al.'s (2000) Canadian study. Mawhinney's (2012) qualitative study used autoethnography and personal narratives to examine the role of othermothering in student-teacher relationships at a historically Black college and university (HBCU). In this study, Mawhinney not only underscored the important role of othermothering as a means of retention and social connection at an HBCU, but also cautions faculty about the boundaries that are needed in such othermothering relationships, as othermothering often requires psychic energy, time, and sometimes financial commitment. This autoethnograpy also discussed the varied experiences of students at the HBCU where othermothering was normative as well as Mawhinney's experience when she began teaching at a predominately White institution (PWI). At the PWI, her experience with othermothering was still present but not necessarily normative and the student-teacher conversation mainly centered on the issue of race.

In Griffin's (2013) study, othermothering was again used to identify how 28 Black faculty members from two public research universities viewed their relationships with Black students. Griffin used social exchange theory to analyze these relationships and found that the interactions were unique in that (a) Black faculty had a sense of obligation to Black students and were committed to their success, and (b) there was a sense of closeness and comfort felt with Black students. These findings are important because they are both components of othermothering, which is supported by Guiffrida's (2005) study on othermothering (Griffin, 2013), and is the central framework for the DIVAS collective. Based on the work of Mawhinney (2012) and Griffin (2013), othermothering as a theoretical and practical lens maps well with the autoenthnographies present in this volume and the important role of relationships, mentoring, and obligation that are central features of the DIVAS framework, which will be discussed later in this introduction.

The previous synthesis of the concept othermothering has been discussed in terms of Black women's psychology (Bryant, 1999) as well as its role in the institutions of higher education both nationally and internationally (Bernard et al., 2000; Griffin, 2013; Mawhinney, 2012), but the applicability of the concept is also relevant to the community work of Black women. In her qualitative study of nine Black women who worked in Black communities and churches, Edwards (2000) used othermothering to expand how the concept unfolds in the everyday work of Black women. She terms this "community mothering" to reflect the historical ways in which Black women define, support, and navigate the work they do in their community. Overall, she found that the concept of community mothering was relevant to lives of women who worked in community organizations such as Parent Teacher Associations and women who worked in the church who saw othermothering as an important aspect of community upliftment and modeling womanhood for younger Black women. An important discussion point for Edwards (2000) is that the women in her study enacted community mothering without expectation of rewards. Similarly, in her study of African American school principals, Loder (2005) found that these women used community othermothering to interact with the community, show love and care for the students and their families, as well as rebuild the community. A central component of the DIVAS collective is our cultural and heuristic understanding of the word "community." The intersectionality between Edwards's (2000) and Loder's (2005) research provides a bridge to the current model of peer-to-peer mentoring that is a key component of the DIVAS success. DIVAS model community in our organization and in our communities; in fact, our mission statement clearly outlines that service to one's community is a central aspect of who we are. In addition, DIVAS as a collective is the quintessential model of community mothering as we mother each other academically and socially without any expectation of compensation.

It is through this epistemology that the DIVAS build our courage and strength. We came to understand that it was because of the courage and strength in our lineage that we were empowering and validating one another. The section that follows details the second concept, fictive kin. Once we became vulnerable with one another and our individual experiences, the bond strengthened to fictive kin by a sisterhood.

Fictive Kin

The second concept with which DIVAS is built is fictive kin (Ebaugh & Curry, 2000; Fordham, 1996), and it is through othermothering that we have become fictive kin. Kinship or fictive kinship is a term that conveys the idea of brotherhood and sisterhood of all African Americans regardless of class, gender, and sexual orientation (Fordham, 1996). Indeed, genuine kinship bonds served as models for affective obligation among non-kin; these responsibilities were then transferred into broader social and communal obligations (Chatters, Taylor, & Jayakody, 1994). Establishing this kind of bond within the wall of the academy over several disciplines has allowed the DIVAS to learn the complexities and unspoken norms of a PhD program.

From this, the DIVAS understand that we must consider the academic, institutional, and social context within which each member is situated if we are to promote our sisters' academic and personal success to become our sisters' keeper. Cook (2010) asserts, "fictive kin encourages an emphasis on the value of cooperation, collaboration, and solidarity" (p. 25). As a result, the intensified kinship bonds of the DIVAS grew as we began to meet monthly and build the trust and mutual obligation we have to one another. What is more, it is through this fictive kinship that we are able to celebrate, laugh, cry, persevere, and find courage as individuals and as a collective.

Another critical aspect of the DIVAS community and survival within the walls of the academy and within our group has been our courageous Christian faith. The section that follows makes sense of the faith that many of the DIVAS carry and why it is so embedded in our many identities.

Faith as Community and Capital

Essentially, for many of the DIVAS our Christian values, foundation, and belief system was our first community. In this first community, we began to build our strength through spiritual and religious Christian values of hope, love, purpose, freedom and long-suffering, and justice. As we became more formalized as a collective we were able to intersect our multiple identities, which allowed us to marry the academic, spiritual, religious, and cultural aspects of our identities and experiences into a narrative that was necessary for survival. The role of faith, particularly its spiritual and religious dimensions in the lives of the Black community, has been highlighted in the extant research literature (Brown & Gary, 1991; Hill, 1972; Jagers & Smith 1996; Mattis & Jagers, 2001; Taylor, 1988), underscoring the important role each plays in socialization and development. Mattis's (2000) study examined the meanings that

African American women ascribe to spirituality and religiosity and forwarded that both constructs are complex and intertwined in the lived experience of the 127 university-enrolled African American women she interviewed.

Analogously, Brown and Gary (1991), in their research on religious socialization and educational attainment, suggest that the church and religiously affiliated activities acted as socializing agents for the African American community. Their research findings suggest that religious socialization can affect educational achievement of African American individuals.

Moreover, Dantley (2005) declares that spirituality in particular has had a long tradition in the African American community and that

> spirituality has served as the catalyst to continue African Americans' quest for equity and equality in a less-than-welcoming culture: African American spirituality is the internal grounding of many Black people's ontology or sense of being. It crafts a sense of self and provides the impetus to resist forms and practices of dehumanization and oppression that are sometimes promoted by the dominant culture. (p. 657)

Cynthia Dillard's (2006) book *On Spiritual Strivings: Transforming an African American Woman's Academic Life* provides a framework for understanding the intersectionality of academic work and personal spirituality, and we extend this to faith practices. She contends, "speaking of a spiritual life and defining spirituality is fraught with difficulty. This is especially true when it comes to speaking of places and spaces that we've traditionally thought of as 'academic'" (Dillard, 2006, p. 40). As a collective we refuse to be defined by epistemologies and worldviews that devalue the role of sacred faith and spiritual spaces and beliefs in our work within the academy and in our communities. Dillard forwards that spiritual strivings for her include daily writings, prayer, and meditation, which centers her work and brings purpose. For the DIVAS our association with faith, spirituality, and religiosity are operationalized in the form of prayer, church attendance, wisdom, biblical precepts, devotions, social-justice-affiliated work, and community engagement. Thus, within the executive body of our organization we have a DIVA chaplin whose role is to keep us spiritually connected to God, our community, and family.

As DIVAS, our spiritual and religious foundation provided and continues to provide a framework of hope for us in an academy that does not value our kind of epistemological, axiological, and ontological framing. As Freire (1994) explains in *Pedagogy of Hope*:

> But without struggle, hope as an ontological need dissipates, loses its bearings, and turns into hopelessness. And hopelessness can become tragic despair. Hence the need for a kind of education is hope. Hope, as it happens, is so important

for our existence, individual and social, that we must take every care not to experience it in a mistaken form, and thereby allow it to slip toward hopelessness
and despair. Hopelessness and despair are both the consequence and the cause of
inaction or immobilism. (p. 9)

Quintessentially, our hope-laden Christian faith functions as a source of resistance against institutional, systemic, and societal ideological and hegemonic
assumptions that often push issues of race, culture, and gender to the margins.
As a result, the collection of stories in this volume reflect the complexities of
women who navigate multiple courageous realities where faith, spirituality,
and religiosity merge in ways that are inseparable, liberating, nuanced, and
central to the mission of the DIVAS collective, as well as our teaching and
learning practices. Generett and Cozart's (2012) work captures the very essence of the role of faith in the lives of the DIVAS. In their article, "The Spirit
Bears Witness: Reflections of Two Black Women's Journey in the Academy,"
they state:

> In our evolution as academics we are now in a place where we recognize that our
> work and ultimate ability to heal from past hurts related to our educational ex-
> periences, does not rest solely in our ability to turn the experience into data and
> evidence, but also in our ability to continually reach back to the spiritual sources
> which got us through and to where we currently are positioned. (p. 18)

Through our stories of courage, hope, and faith, the DIVAS are able to represent a naturalistic embodiment of the daily realities of the lives of a group
of Black women who are grounded by faith and bound together through the
common experience of Black women in academe. Our work is emancipatory,
courageous, and liberatory because "coherence is realized in our collective
refusal to be reduced to someone else's terms: To give voice to silenced spaces
as an act of resistance" (Dillard, 2006, p. 19). In each DIVAS narrative, you
will see that the women have moved from our common Christian faith experiences in order to provide counter-narratives that will help all women examine
their identities as women in the academy, and as women of spirit, faith, and
hope. We borrow from Maya Angelou's poem "Still I Rise," because the stories in this volume represent the hope and courage of the slaves.

Claiming Our Legacy

For the DIVAS the process of obtaining a doctorate has transformed into
a journey for knowledge as well as empowerment, voice, commitment, and
relationships. Essentially, our journey and experiences are sustained in what
Rochelle Brock (2005) terms the third space. She states:

> I worked in the third space of indigenous knowledge, which kept me grounded in my own positionality. It is this space that allows me to put my Black femaleness at the center of the search for knowledge. Here is where I can begin to know myself, and Black women, by asking and searching for the answers to ontological questions of existence. I place the knowledge created by my Black sisters at the fore. The third space is where I live and learn, stretch and breathe. (p. xvi)

Within the DIVAS narrative we clearly embody and represent an epistemology that is grounded in the work of other Black women academics such as Patricia Hill Collins, bell hooks, Rochelle Brock, and Cynthia Dillard. We borrow from Cynthia Dillard's (2006) work, in which she unpacks her concept of an endarkened feminist epistemology. According to Dillard, "in defining an endarkened feminist epistemology, I deliberately sought language that attempts to unmask traditionally held political and cultural constructions/constrictions, language that more accurately organizes, resists, and transforms oppressive descriptions of sociocultural phenomena and relationships" (p. 2). We also tap into the essence of life given us from our mamas, grandmamas, aunts, church elders, and the conventional females around the way. As such, we make no apology for centering issues of race, gender, class, and faith in our academic experiences. Based on our collective experiences, we fully understand our role in confronting hegemony and ideologies that attempt to silence our voices as Black women. What follows is the history of the DIVAS collective along with the structure and makeup of our organization.

Birthing, Bolts, and Breaking Out: The Anatomy of the DIVAS

Birthing: The Beginning of DIVAS

The initial DIVAS meeting was held on September, 27, 2009, at 7:00 pm. The founding members of DIVAS came from several academic disciplines including teacher education (5), higher education (5), educational leadership and foundations (1), and specialized educational services (1). The process of maneuvering the doctoral program had become isolating, discontenting, frustrating, and misleading to navigate, thus an informal conversation between two (Toni and Cherrel) gave rise to the meeting of this group of dynamic Black women.

Dialogue about what was going well and areas that required attention, a sense of belonging, commitment, and sisterhood were immediately central constructs at this first meeting as we fully realized that we were embarking on and creating a counter-narrative in an academy that is patriarchal and Eurocentric. We understood that we were embodying Collins's (1989) statement, "for Black women, new knowledge claims are rarely worked out in isolation from other individuals and are usually developed through dialogues with others of the community" (p. 763). Maintaining dialogue has allowed the DIVAS to establish a place for Black women doctoral students and emerging scholars to create a community.

The collective has now expanded to include members from the nursing, rhetoric and composition, and educational research methods disciplines. Currently the sisterhood has a membership including more than 20 doctoral students, faculty, and administrators in higher education in four states. The DIVAS understand that the experiences of Black women in academia are very complex and nuanced. As such, our mission is to *empower Black women in the academy by providing mentoring as well as academic and research support to enhance scholarship and community involvement.*

As noted earlier, the collective was formed as a result of a conversation between Cherrel Miller Dyce, currently DIVAS' president, and Toni Milton Williams, DIVAS' vice president, which was precipitated by unnerving events that surrounded the comprehensive exam of Milton Williams. That event formed a bond between DIVAS Cherrel and Toni that produced a sisterhood of healing, purpose, vision, and hope. It was during one of our daily conversations that DIVA Toni asked the question, "I wonder how many other Black women have experienced what happened to me?" From this life-changing statement, Toni and Cherrel decided to reach out to and assemble Black women on the campus to simply talk. At the initial meeting we recognized that we had come together out of a need for one another in our current academic situations. We knew that this was a journey that required the help of the village, not just one individual; thus, the bond of kinship and the DIVAS premise that "none would be lost" originated.

Bolts: The Way DIVAS Roll

Like other organizations, the DIVAS have a formal governing structure that includes a president, vice president, secretary, treasurer, chaplin, public relations officer, historian, and various coordinators for membership, outreach, technology, and professional development. The DIVAS collective operates within eight essential components from our framework:

1. Flexibility. We are a voluntary and fluid group. Members come to the group on their own accord and can vacillate in and out to DIVAS as warranted by their life circumstances.

2. Affinity. We are bound together by a spiritual and social connection. Each meeting includes prayer, praise, and meditation, often led by the DIVAS chaplin.

3. Cooperation. We work in collaboration, not competition with each other to produce quality scholarship and we push one another towards academic excellence. We frequently meet for work sessions to write together, discuss current research, or for a social event. Furthermore, the DIVAS collaborate for local and national conference presentations along with our annual DIVAS conference at Elon University.

4. Our charge is to recognize our responsibility to those who have come before us and those who will come after us. We are therefore committed to contributing to our community by investing our time, gifts, and talents.

5. Dedication. The DIVAS will provide for each other a consistent support network of accountability and responsibility through critical conversations.

DIVAS FRAMEWORK

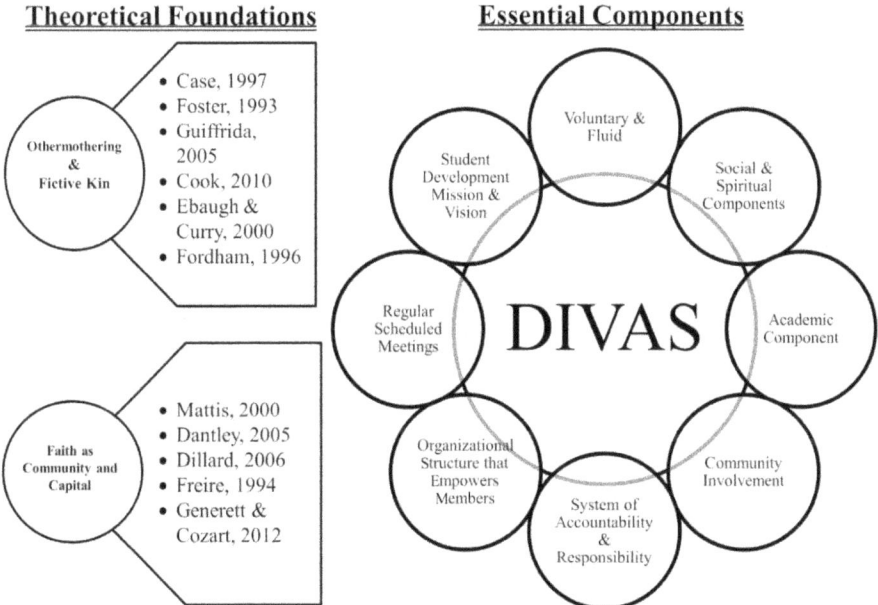

We have a peer-mentoring model in which senior DIVAS (those who have crossed over) are paired with junior DIVAS (those in the doctoral process) for more intense academic grooming.

6.   Our organizational structure allows for members to share in the creative process of keeping the collective relevant, rooted and rigorous in our research, scholarship, and service. In this way, DIVAS hold various leadership positions inside and outside of the organization as well as within our respective communities.

7.   We hold regular monthly scheduled meetings to discuss matters of business and to join in fellowship with one another. Each meeting is driven with purpose and promise as we solicit advice from one another and challenge ourselves as scholars. The standard at all meetings is to keep DIVA business at DIVA meetings.

8.   We maintain a holistic approach and believe in the academic, institutional, and social context of teaching and learning. We believe that we are responsible for empowering one another to succeed against all odds.

These eight philosophical bolts form the catalyst for merging the personal and the pedagogical (Brock, 2005). A coming together of minds for DIVAS has been vital in maintaining relationships. Bettez (2011) states, "For the most part, the academic work is a lonely process. We read alone, most often write alone, usually teach alone, and frequently think and process alone" (p. 9). Thus, the culture of working together and sharing academic air has been stimulating, as we have discussions on theorists, researchers, and terminology, and dream about how we can inspire one another with spiritual uplift. At any given time in our sessions, it is not uncommon for one to break out in a song of inspiration, do a dance for victory and accomplishments, share a narrative from one's personal life, or a simple cry for comfort and support. This kind of camaraderie is what allows each DIVA to express herself in a culturally safe academic community and build solidarity. In fact, Beauboeuf-Lafontant (2009) suggests, "The defining quality of Black womanhood is strength" (p. 1). We gain strength from our coming together, as we oftentimes laugh, cry, and join together in a spiritual realm, which further strengthens our sisterhood.

Breaking Out: How Far DIVAS Have Come

"Women of color come in a variety of hues, they are rare, and they need polishing for their brilliance to shine through" (Bowen, 2012, p. 132). Three years after the inception of our group, we have gone from one DIVA, Cherrel Miller Dyce, who completed her PhD, to more than 12 polished Doctor DIVAS, an affectionate term in our organization for PhD completers. DIVAS now are *breaking out* into institutions of higher education and non-profits across the country as faculty and administrators. We are living the original statement from our first meeting that "we are the Black face of education for tomorrow." The driving force in our collective is that we continue to mentor other Black women and each other in navigating the cultural, social, and historical turning points of the academy. In this manner, DIVAS continue to remain connected, despite distance. Staying true to our framework of fluidity and voluntary participation, DIVAS remain connected to each other through our monthly meetings where members join the conversation through various technological modalities such as Skype and conference calls. It is not uncommon to receive a message on our DIVAS email list of a member seeking guidance regarding her career, prayer, or just sharing accomplishments.

As we have grown as an organization, we continue to share our stories within our local communities, and our membership body is steadily increasing as other Black women seek a lifeline in the often-lonely PhD process. This is important, because often we receive requests for membership based on other faculty referring their students. The counter-narratives we embody are no longer on the periphery; they are now at the center of our teaching and learning processes. As a result, the DIVAS collective truly believes in the emancipatory power of teaching and learning for social justice, for ourselves and others. We balance this with bell hooks's (1994) belief that

> To educate as the practice of freedom is a way of teaching that anyone can learn. That learning process comes easiest to those of us who teach who also believe that there is an aspect of our vocation that is sacred; who believe that our work is not merely to share information but to share in the intellectual and spiritual growth of our students. (p. 13)

This book creates a space for the DIVAS to *break out* in terms of scholarship, community, and transformation of the very nature of higher education; yet we remain dedicated to one another beyond the walls of the academy. As we unfold as an organization, we are breaking out and challenging our sisters at other institutions to create their own communities in order that they may *break out* as well. As a collective, our stories provide substance, courage, and integrity to the narrative of the Black woman academic. Further, we provide insights to those individuals who are not familiar with our trajectory and want to gain a better understanding of the ways in which we navigate our paths.

The purpose of this book is to introduce the higher education community to a model of an effective peer-to-peer mentoring and support group that can aid in doctoral retention and completion for Black women doctoral students. This book serves as a model and affirmation that as Black women making sense of our world and that of the academy, we can maintain success. We demonstrate the importance of building and associating with a community capable of othermothering and fictive kin relationships. We take you through our stories with metaphors and transitions that speak to the essence of who we are as individuals and as a collective. We share with you our idiosyncrasies, letdowns, setbacks, successes, and celebrations through various theoretical lenses, voices, and experiences.

The scope of *DIVAS Diaries* is far reaching. Not only can *DIVAS Diaries* be utilized as academic text, but it also serves as a retention tool for graduate schools, admissions departments, multicultural centers, and doctoral mentoring programs. This edited volume will cover all aspects of the doctoral process as contributors discuss their personal multifaceted realities as these collide with the academic culture and expectations of doctoral programs. Furthermore, *DIVAS Diaries* can be used as a practical, student-centered sourcebook for Black women doctoral students to navigate the halls of higher education. It is a personal look at the victories and trials through sociocultural, political, economic, historical, and international lenses.

The narratives in this anthology were formed out of our collective experiences and thereby forward new research in the form of a collective counter-narrative (what we call "Black-centric critical consciousness") often not found in doctoral programs, which can be individualistic, lone-wolf settings. Overall, *DIVAS Diaries* is our attempt to othermother Black women entering the academy as well as those seeking a doctoral degree. Sistas, our labor of love is for you.

Pursuing Courage

By Cherrel Miller Dyce

Daughters of the morning come forth
Sistas of purpose arise
Take your rightful places
Claim your freedom
Celebrate your heroic lineage—Mama, Tubman, Nanny, Truth,
Feel their embrace as they light your path to liberation
Smile, Embrace, Live, Love, Laugh, Believe, Build, Possess

Meditations and Deliberations on DIVAS

Toni Milton Williams and Cherrel Miller Dyce

In the four years since our inception, DIVAS has developed discourse that represents the culture that we've established, which Bettez (2011) describes this way:

> Creating a sense of community to promote collective teaching and learning, in which peers who are more versed in the academic discourse and academic codes of power are encouraged to use multivocality to assist less experienced students, can minimize individuals' self-doubts in their learning abilities and promote success for all, rather than maintain understanding only among a few. (p. 11)

We begin by sharing our DIVAS world with you, the reader, in hopes that you will get a glimpse into how the DIVAS connect with one another, building a supportive and safe community.

DIVAS (de: vuz) n. Black women in pursuit of a PhD, a friend, sister, writing partner, source of strength and support; a place of refuge from academia that fosters collaboration, an authentic, organic group of Black women who laugh, cry, challenge one another, love and nurture each other.

DIVA utterings: Terms and sayings that DIVAS have dubbed since being established

- **DIVA LUV:** Signifies the bond that has been created, how DIVAS show love.
- **Big DIVA Sis/Little DIVA Sis:** A means of mentoring one another within the group.
- **OD:** Original DIVA, a founding DIVA.

- **Crossing over:** A DIVA who has obtained her PhD.
- **Praise report:** Sharing good news with the group.
- **Lock and Rock:** Holding hands, symbolizes the strength of the group to support one another and grow together. During meetings DIVAS often lock hands and rock back and forth to demonstrate the power and strength in our collective.
- **Dr. DIVAS:** DIVAS on the other side of the process, who have completed their PhD.
- **Sista DIVAS:** DIVAS preparing to graduate.
- **Sista Circle:** Production groups, including writing groups (Dr. DIVAS toward tenure or Sista DIVAS toward completion); it is all about accountability.
- **DW/DIVAS writing group:** Accountability partners = the person who holds you accountable for writing, and you them; it is all about production for a specific purpose; we say what we need and someone steps up to meet them.
- **DIGS:** DIVAS interest group with similar interests and pathways; forms ideas and supports you as you go along (i.e., topics on Black males) sharing articles, going to conference.
- **DIVALICIOUS:** A dynamic idea, thought, plan.

DIVAS Speak: Expressions from the DIVA community

- "You all are a powerful example of the power of collectivity and determination." — **Dr. Silvia Bettez,** *DIVAS conference keynote speaker*
- "I believe in DIVAS and what we stand for." — **DIVA Torry Reynolds**
- "The DIVAS refused to let me fail. My DIVA Sistas embraced me; I embraced them right back, and I am better as a result." — **DIVA Dawn Tafari**
- Like any family DIVAS is made up of many disciplines, backgrounds, and ideologies. It is this uniqueness that causes us to be such a dynamic and multifaceted collective. If you ask me what DIVAS has meant to me it's simple, *SISTERHOOD.* If you ask me one word I would use to describe us that is even easier, *PROUD.* — **DIVA LaWanda Wallace**
- The unparalleled wisdom, support, and opportunities offered through this female PhD cohort helps to strengthen the lives of its graduate and post-graduate members. DIVAS is an impactful, meaningful, organic structure formed out of sheer necessity to meet the needs of

underserved demographics who are earning the highest degree attainable within the educational system. In its very inception, DIVAS represents what is considered a "transformative educational paradigm" that highlights the purpose of educational involvement: "the evolution of multidimensional identity, including but not limited to cognitive, affective, behavioral and spiritual development" (Keeling, 2004, p. 9).
— **DIVA Temeka Carter**

- DIVAS paralleled my PhD journey and provided a venue in which a collective of like-minded individuals convened to engage in scholarly efforts related to research and teaching. Also important to the mission of DIVAS is the focus on service and leaving the world in better condition. The sisterhood nurtured opportunities for members (or should I say "me"?) to present at professional conferences and audiences from varied disciplines. For me, DIVAS made all the difference in my successful matriculation and career. — **DIVA Cynthia Wooten**

- DIVAS provided me with theoretically grounded support and encouragement that was valuable yet different from what I had received from my doctoral program. Anchored in the tenets of *Learning Reconsidered* (Keeling, 2004) and the community traditions of connectedness through mutual *othermothering* (Foster, 1993; Guiffrida, 2005), I learned skills and gained confidence needed for navigating the doctoral process. I was able to draw strength to complete my program (and so have many others), which is the chief aim of DIVAS. — **DIVA Cynthia Shamberger**

- It was affirming to know that I was NOT the only one struggling through some of the issues related to my academic growth. Before my first presentation of my research at a national conference, I presented before my DIVA sistas and received valuable feedback that aided in my preparation for the conference presentation. DIVA support and prayer at my dissertation defense was powerful! I'll never forget the love and concern displayed. — **DIVA Kim Pemberton**

1. *Standing in the Gap as the Academic Intercessor*

Cherrel Miller Dyce

Exodus: Jamaica to the PhD

Without a doubt, my journey to the doctorate has been influenced by the nature and structure of my community and family. My perspective on education has been forged and influenced by immigration, communal reciprocity, cultural flexibility, family involvement and dedication, a robust work ethic, Jamaican national pride, and my faith. Quintessentially, my educational odyssey is a classic example of Bronfenbrenner's (1979) ecological systems theory where constructs such as interdependency, collectivity, reciprocity, and mutuality are correlated with intrapsychic well-being and self-worth.

From an early age, I witnessed the power of the collective in promoting the physical, socio-emotional, cultural, and economical survival of not only micro-level constituencies but members in the meso and macro systems as well. My grandmother, a valorous advocate in our community, was years ahead of her time in situating issues of social justice outside of individual-level characteristics. Ostensibly, my grandmother, a farmer in rural Jamaica, lived and embodied central components of Africentrism, a worldview that is centered in the experiences of individuals of African descent in the Diaspora, valuing concepts such as harmony, balance, oneness, and interconnectedness (Hunn, 2004). Concomitantly, I saw others in my family and community—mother, aunts, grandfather, and teachers—use the very complex biological tools of the mind, eyes, ears, mouth, heart, hands, and feet to assist, restore, bear, and renew others in the community. In other words, they stood in the gap practicing communalism, spirituality, and humanity, all aspects of an Africentric worldview (Hunn, 2004). Such a worldview and an understanding of the concept of community is a central underpinning of why DIVAS was formed.

Patricia Hill Collins (2010) reminds us "the construct of community constitutes both a principle of actual social organization and an idea that people use to make sense of and shape their everyday lived realities" (p. 8). Since Jacqueline Fleming's (1984) seminal book, *Blacks in College*, there has been what I call a "naming" or clarion call, underscoring the nuanced experiences of Black students (and I would add faculty, a world I now inhabit) in institutions of higher education, particularly in predominately White institutions. Many in the scholarly community (Dowdy, 2008; Holmes, Land, & Hinton-Hudson, 2007; Jones, Wilder, & Osborne-Lampkin, 2013; Patton & Harper, 2003) have written about the realities of "being a fly in the buttermilk" (Davis et al., 2004, p. 420), inhabiting academic spaces and identities that can often be incongruent with the very nature of what the concept of community upholds. One such chronicle is a study by Gildersleeve, Croom, and Vasquez (2011), who problematized the experiences of Black and Latino doctoral students using a critical race theory paradigm and centered their results and discussion in a framework that asked the question, "Am I going crazy?"—a phrase borrowed from one of their participants who expressed the cultural and social dissonance experienced in the doctoral process. So, instead of the doctoral process representing an academic marriage or a state of psychological R. E. M.—reciprocity, emotionality, and mutuality (Albold & Miller Dyce, 2011), it can be a convector of insecurity, isolation, and academic suicide, all wrapped in a nice package called success. Instead of embodying what should be a communal birthing (Nerad & Miller, 1997), the road to the PhD is often littered with actors labeled as ABD—all but dissertation. The data on PhD completion for Black women represents a pipeline where between Reconstruction and the dawning of WWII, fewer than 400 African Americans received doctoral degrees (Thompson, 1999), and although the attainment of doctoral degrees by Black and other women of color are increasing, their attainment is still lower than their counterparts (Gildersleeve et al., 2011).

It is within this framework of underrepresentation that a spark ignited the creation of DIVAS, a concept birthed from the very souls of DIVAS co-president Toni Milton Williams and me, with the vision that "none would be lost," that we (Black women on the PhD journey) would be dissertation completers and overcomers, even if we had to cross the finish line on broken pieces. DIVAS echo Shirley Jackson, past president of the Rensselaer Polytechnic Institute, and the sentiment she expressed in her address on women of color in science, technology, and math: "as scholars, we must inspire by example. As mothers, we must inspire by cultivating the next generation of achievers. As sisters, we must continue to build our networks and organizations of inspirational support." (1999, p. 28). In 1903, W. E. B. Du Bois penned *The Souls of Black Folk,* in which he stated, "we the darker ones come even now not altogether empty-handed: there are to-day no truer exponents of the pure human spirit of the Declaration of Independence than the American Negroes" (p. 15). DIVAS, as a collective, embodies the declaration and fortitude that the whole is greater than its parts; that when individuals come together as a collective body, capital is produced for collective transformation. For members of the DIVAS collective, our capital is embedded in our conceptual framework and its components, which include: being voluntary and fluid; fostering social and spiritual connections; collaborating in academic support; providing community involvement; working within a system of accountability and responsibility; empowering organizational structure; holding regular meetings; and the development of the entire student/member.

Although my experience as a doctoral student was one that included stumbling blocks, it was also a very positive and transformational experience as a result of the excellent mentorship of my committee chairs and the legacy of "standing in the gap" that was modeled for me as a young girl. Felder (2010), in her research on faculty mentoring of African American doctoral students, found that faculty mentoring can aid in socialization, and faculty mentors who are collaborative and who combat and help mitigate the feelings of isolation and marginality can help improve the doctoral climate for disenfranchised students. But what about other Black women who are seeking someone to help them achieve a degree that only a small percentage of the population possesses? President Obama, in his 2008 Democratic Party Nomination Acceptance Speech, said it well when he declared, "Born into poverty? Pull yourself up by your own bootstraps—even if you don't have boots. You are on your own" (para. 22). This propensity toward individualism has dominated the American ideological landscape for decades. For Black women pursuing a PhD, will there be anyone to stand in the gap to assist them in making the doctorate a reality when the doctoral landscape is littered by obstacles (Felder, 2010)? Will there be anyone to lend a boot, intercede, and model success in an academy where Black women represent a small percentage of the population? Will there be anyone to perform what Guiffrida (2005) calls othermothering, a concept denoting the role of mentoring, support, and connection in the academic persistence of African American students?

Broadly, this chapter will tell the story of how DIVAS was formed; it will detail my role as what I call an academic intercessor, a concept that intersects spirituality within the academic mentoring process. I will situate this concept within the theories of Black feminist thought, othermothering, and a concept from my dissertation known as village network. Last, I will conclude with the importance of coalition building and solidarity as pedagogies of persistence and endurance for Black women doctoral students.

Genesis: The Making of the DIVAS Collective

I entered my predominately White doctoral program with a kaleidoscope of emotions that oscillated between two polar dimensions. On one hand was the fear of academic and social failure (Gildersleeve et al., 2011), as well as disappointing my family and community, and on the other hand were hopes, optimism, pride, and the dreams of countless Blacks in the Diaspora who view education as a vehicle for social uplift and transformation. L. R. Jackson (1998) also discovered in her study of race, gender, and the experiences of African American women at four college campuses across the country, that self-perception is affected by the racial and gender composition of the college. Jackson (1998) uncovered three themes from her participants and their experiences at predominately White institutions: the participants felt that (1) being an African American woman meant struggle, (2) being an African American woman can be problematic, and (3) being an African American woman meant being conscious. Despite this kind of triple consciousness, I continued to pursue the doctorate with hooks's (1994) position that education is a practice of freedom. Most of all, I carried the quest for freedom in every paper I wrote, every presentation I gave, every discussion with faculty, and during each new semester. Although I was a product of an Ivy League education, the road to the doctorate was one seeded with uncertainties, as well as an unrelenting pedagogy of possibilities. I knew that I was the academic social capital for my family and community, as I would be the first on both sides of my family and one of the few from my small community in Jamaica to earn a doctorate.

When I started my doctorate in the Higher Education Administration, I was one of two Black women in my program at a predominately White institution in the Southern part of the United States. The other Black woman was from the South and I had just relocated from the Northeast. She was enrolled part-time and I was enrolled full-time and was the graduate assistant for my small department. I remember the first day of class, looking around at my cohort and wondering, "Can I do this?" and despite the developmental theories that purported individuation in the college process, my academic self-efficacy, as well as my identity as a Black woman on a predominately White campus, was a salient reminder of my responsibility to my community. The intersectionality of my race, gender, social class, and academic sense of self resulted in a convergence that challenged hegemony and ideological assumptions but also produced hesitations in terms of my academic prowess in the classroom. These experiences were very similar to ones expressed by the participants in Gildersleeve et al.'s (2011) study. To further examine this kind of intersectionality, Viernes Turner's (2002) research on women of color and marginality in academia begins with her own personal testimony:

> I recall a personal example of how multiple social identities may shape one's opportunity in higher education … the admission officer stated that I would not fit in. I was a woman, a minority, a single parent, I had a background in the public sector, and I had some but not enough math background. (p. 74)

Understanding marginality and intersectionality in the student experience is important, and like Viernes Turner's (2002) research, *Learning Reconsidered*, a document crafted by two of the leading student-affairs organizations also calls for an understanding of the personal, historical, and sociocultural factors that affect learning in and out of the classroom (Keeling, 2004).

Throughout my educational career, I had always been a diligent and good student; however, my journey to the PhD unearthed a narrative and inner conflict that supports the research on stereotype threat (Steele, 1997; Taylor & Anthony, 2000). Steele's (1997) research on stereotype threat was a reality for me as I struggled with my multiple responsibilities of being a mother, wife, mentor, granddaughter, and daughter, while remaining present in the classroom in ways that caused dissonance, critical reflections, self-doubt, and a constant state of double consciousness. Despite my fears, I knew failure was not an option. I knew that my role was to create an environment with fewer stumbling blocks for the unknown and faceless Black sisters who would follow. In an academy that often devalues non-European ways of knowing, I maintained my responsibility to the collective, which was my anchor throughout the doctoral process as I held on to my collectivist foundations and my social networks in order to balance my experiences and identity in the academic arena. My personal epistemological, axiological, and ontological propeller provided the movement I needed to transgress (hooks, 1994) the boundaries of educational hegemony and see education as a practice of freedom and hope (Freire, 1992, 1994).

Hence, as my studies progressed and I began to show mastery in written and verbal assessments, as well as establish myself as a leader and social support in my program, my emotions began to gain permanence on the positive end of the academic pole. I was able to master the art of conscientization (Freire, 1992) and recognized the importance of positionality in the academy. As I became exposed to the work of bell hooks, Paulo Freire, Patricia Hill

Collins, Cornel West, John Ogbu, Beverly Tatum, and others in the critical theory tradition, I began to create an academic space that did not seem so threatening.

This all changed during the final semester of my studies. I had successfully completed my comprehensive exam and defended them orally with a flare that made my mother, my greatest advocate, and now-deceased grandmother proud. I had already completed the final draft of my dissertation and was awaiting my time to defend, just as I was awaiting the birth of my third child within a few weeks. In the four years of my studies, I and others had created a community we called "the doc office"—the shared space inhabited by many doctoral students nationwide. This kind of out-of-classroom environment was transformational and integral to the doctoral experience because it was a location where learning was truly reconsidered (Keeling, 2004). This shared space created a holistic environment where class lectures, readings, and programmatic concerns were discussed in the safety of peers. The experiences of doctoral students are complex and nuanced. More specifically, the type of mentoring and support one receives frames the type of outcomes possible. Patton and Harper (2003), in their research underscoring the importance of mentoring relationships for African American women in graduate studies, state that mentoring is a key factor in academic and career success. In a similar manner, Brown, Davis, and McClendon (1999) encourage institutions of higher education to design mentoring program that will not only help maintain students of color, but recognize the institutional factors that prevent success. Conversely, my friend and colleague from "the doc office" reached a place of reckoning in the doctoral process that was very difficult, torrid, and life changing, challenging the innermost fabric of her soul. She was enrolled in the Teacher Education Program and, as noted earlier, I was enrolled in the Higher Education Administration program. We shared space in "the doc office" as both programs were housed within the same department, and we often took certain classes together, discussed issues of Blackness in the academy, as well as our role in dismantling oppression and as agents of change for our community. As I and others waited anxiously in the office, she walked down the hall to defend the dreaded comprehensive exam—a rite of passage for all who embark on this process. As we waited patiently like jubilant parents, we realized that the comprehensive defense was taking longer than usual. My mind began to perform robotics, and the fears that encapsulated me throughout the program came back like a mighty rushing wind. As I ventured to the bathroom with my very pregnant body, I was greeted with a remark that arrested time forever. A fellow student said, "Cherrel, I saw Toni in the hall and she was waiting against the wall." It became very clear that the committee was not pleased with the process. As I waited for her in our shared office space, I realized that something was drastically wrong. My heart began to beat when I saw one of the committee members come to the office and ask for her coat. I wobbled out of the office as fast as I would run. When I reached her, her silent brokenness was spilling over without any indication of release—this was not a case of communal birthing (Nerad & Miller, 1997). She was not approved and would have to do some more work in order to fully pass her comprehensive exam. This was a devastating day for her and for all present as they, too, understood that one day soon they would have to walk alone to the dreaded oral comprehensive examination defense.

As she and I gathered together for strength on the couch in my living room a few hours after her comprehensive exam, we knew that we were in it together. We cried and comforted each other that day as the pain opened old wounds that were too much for one to bear. As the tears rolled down our faces, and as we bowed our heads in silence while looking through my living-room windows, our spirit and soul connected and awakened the academic intercessor in me that would help to stand in the gap. My living room, with its vibrant colors reminiscent of the beautiful Caribbean sea and my small Jamaican village, became a conduit for what is now DIVAS' framework of othermothering. Othermothering, a tool of healing and retention, began that day as Toni and I called on the strength and philosophies of the Black teachers in Foster's (1993) study to be our balm. Like the changes in the seasons, the weeks after brought forth the hope of spring and provoked a reawakening of our linked spirits. Consequently, the birth of my third child and my successful defense of my dissertation provided us with a fervor and victory that we had not experienced in our academic journey. Toni's comprehensive exam disappointment, coupled with our experience as Black women in the academy, was the impetus for the formation of DIVAS. As we began to unpack our experience in the program, Toni said to me in one of our daily conversations after her comprehensive exam, "I wonder how many Black women have had this experience in their doctoral program?" It was that day that we decided to ask for a gathering of Black women doctoral students from across the campus. Our experience is very similar to the one told by Robinson (1999) regarding her experience at Peabody College. Based on her struggles in the doctoral program at Peabody College, Robinson used a similar strategy to create a mentoring program for students of color at her institutions. She states:

> this is a story of my struggles as a Black female doctoral student attempting to adjust to a new environment. It is a story I have been waiting and wanting to tell for 5 years. This story is meant to inspire those who believe they cannot change or have an impact on their institution or environment, and it is also meant to

make those interested in change aware of the obstacles and tools needed to overcome them. (p. 119)

Utilizing Coleman's (1988) social capital concept of information channels,
we contacted women we both knew by telephone and email and asked them
to invite other Black women to our first meeting.

Our first meeting was held in the fall of 2009, and when Toni told her
story, the room was filled with silence and a sea of tears. We had all connected
on a level that words could not express—the collective unconsciousness. We
decided that day in the halls of academe, Black women from different coun-
tries of origin, social class, cultural backgrounds, and academic programs,
that "none shall be lost." Essentially, this gathering allowed us the safety to
unmask our identities and as Rodriquez (2006) declares,

> unmasking the experiences of women of color is critical in exposing truths that so
> often are guided by the dominant discourse. For women of color, writing about
> our collective histories and experiences, or writing about "theory in the flesh," is
> a necessity for our liberation. (p. 1071)

From this gathering, we decided that we held social and cultural capital that
could be galvanized for action. For us, the personal became political, as we
decided to mentor each other through the process and thereby provide a
model of peer-to-peer mentoring that other Black women in doctoral programs can utilize for purposeful action. This is how the DIVAS collective was
created, from the yearning of our spirits. In her article, "A Visitation from the
Foremothers: Black Women's Healing Through a 'Performance of Care'—
From African Diaspora to the American Academy," Olga Davis (2008) asked
this question: "from what in the academy do Black women need healing?" I
posit that DIVAS was created as a place of healing and will continue to be a
balm for those who have suffered from what my colleague Dr. Buffie Long-
mire-Avital calls "academic amputations," and are now making use of their
prosthetics.

Chronicles: The Making of an Academic Intercessor

Theories have been used to explain human nature for centuries. Often, theories become the foci for understanding phenomena. Theories can be based in
research, personal observations, and lived experiences, as well as teaching and
learning. Undoubtedly, the dialectics of theorizing is a practice of creating
knowledge that is seeded in constructivist ways of knowing. Brock (2005)
contends that:

> It is in the dialectics and dichotomies that Black women search for truth and a deeper meaning of existence. The internal dialectics of Black women are the strength we have historically shown in the face of insurmountable odds as well as our acquiescence to a hegemonic force, which devalues, degrades, dehumanizes, and kills. We are simultaneously strong and weak and in order to understand Black women, one must discover both sides of the dialectic. (p. xvii)

Thus, separating the theory from the theorizer is a futile mission that is bootstrapped with misconceptions. It is with sanguinity that I forward a lens for understanding the anatomy of the makings of an academic intercessor. Essentially, my role as an academic intercessor was born from a personal space, one that is inextricably and forever linked to the creation of the DIVAS collective, as well as our theoretical frameworks of othermothering. In my role as an academic intercessor, I feel very connected to Cynthia Dillard's (2006) work on spirituality in the academic. She states:

> as more and more African-ascendant scholars are immersing ourselves in cultural and spiritual spaces that are congruent with what we know (in body, mind, and spirit), we are also constructing more informed and authentic paradigms for ourselves, paradigms that allows us to emerge from and necessarily transgress the boundaries and norms of conventional social science. (p. 34)

The paradigm of an academic intercessor is my contribution to the canon of literature that centers race, gender, class, and faith in the academy. In understanding what an academic intercessor is or how to embody this quality in the doctoral process or in the academy, one must understand that the concept of an academic intercessor is both a noun and verb. An academic intercessor is who one is (experiences) and what one does (action). So, an academic intercessor inhabits a space of othermothering, which allows for mentoring to not only include academic knowledge, but spiritual leanings and yearnings as well. In forwarding the concept of an academic intercessor, I borrow from myriad research conducted on the role of mentoring for women of color (Brown, Davis, & McClendon, 1999; Holmes, Land, & Hinton-Hudson, 2007; Patton & Harper, 2003; Robinson, 1999) as well as the research on the role of spiritually (Cozart, 2010; Dillard, 2006) and acknowledge that the concept of an academic intercessor is a postmodernist perspective that accounts for multiple truths. Kilgore (2004) reminds us that postmodernists offer multiple truths and "can help us to understand the arbitrary nature of our assumptions about the way people are or ought to be, by offering alternative understandings" (p. 46). Like Howard-Hamilton (2003), who used black feminist thought and critical race theory to articulate the experiences of African American women in higher education, the concept of the academic intercessor is another framework to increase academic and social success of Black women doctoral students.

Thus, in the academy, being an academic intercessor is an inquiry stance that involves the individual's faith and academic history, as well as an understanding of academic knowledge and processes. This is essentially what Patricia Hills Collins posits as the outsider-within relationship (Collins, 1986). Culturally conscious Black women in the academy realize that we are in a warzone where our narratives and epistemologies are often incongruent with the hegemonic, patriarchal, and the Eurocentric academic canon that often tries to silence Black women's unique positionality within the academy. To deconstruct the role of an academic intercessor is to understand that "the emerging Black Feminist literature reveals that many Black intellectuals, especially those in touch with their marginality in academic settings, tap this standpoint in producing distinctive analyses of race, class, and gender" (Collins, 1986, p. 15). An academic intercessor provides a counter-narrative that focuses on an individual or a community's strength instead of the deficit. As such, the actions of an academic intercessor represent the amalgamation of theory and practice-praxis. Theories that influenced my current role as an academic intercessor are situated within the canon of Black feminist thought (Collins, 1986, hooks, 1984, 1994), critical theory (Freire 1992, 1994; Garvey, 1983), othermothering (Guiffrida, 2005), and village network (Miller Dyce, 2009).

Within the DIVAS collective and generally, an academic intercessor is concerned with moving Black women doctoral students from the margin to the center (hooks, 1984) as they progress through doctoral studies. In this manner, the academic intercessor embodies the eight conceptual bolts from our framework, and intercedes in the academic realm with peer-to-peer academic support, such as helping other doctoral students learn the culture of the program and department, serving as reviewers for written work, and providing a space where others can practice presentations and public speeches. The academic intercessor is a constant catalyst for modeling the unwritten rules of the academy and should have an outsider-within (Collins, 1986) perspective about the doctoral process. An academic intercessor must be a leader who is able to articulate a vision and motivate others to act in the face of academic failure or disappointments. In this manner, the academic intercessor must have excellent time-management skills, as standing in the gap requires physical, psychological, and emotional laboring, transference, and lamentation.

Analogously, the academic intercessor performs the duty of othermothering (Case, 1997; Foster, 1993; Guiffrida, 2005). Although DIVAS borrow from Foster's (1993) and Case's (1997) work on othermothering, we center our theoretical framework on Guiffrida's (2005) research as it specifically centers othermothering within institutions of higher education. According to Guiffrida (2005), faculty who are othermothers in the academy are considered student-centered and see their duties as going beyond the basic requirement. Othermothering is another characteristic of an academic intercessor, one who labors with other Black women doctoral students and goes beyond the surface in order to build true connections. If one plans to utilize the theory of othermothering as a lens, one must also understand that the academic intercessor values mentoring and relationships as pillars of academic persistence. As a result, othermothering also provides the academic intercessor with a tool that can aid in retention and belonging in the doctoral process. A central component of the interceding process is to promote academic success of all Black women and to coach them towards completion, thereby upholding our DIVAS motto that "none will be lost." Within the DIVAS, othermothering allows us to search the hall of academe spiritually for our Black sisters, helping to lead them to the crossing.

Continuing the canon, the academic intercessor also belongs to a village network (Miller Dyce, 2009). Village networks are social networks that produce social capital for the sociopolitical, economic, and cultural advancement of an individual, group, or community. Village networks can be an individual's family, faith-based organization, the community, school or other educational institution, and health and mental health agencies. When one stands in the gap as an academic intercessor, one provides support in areas of needed support for other Black women doctoral students in order for them to succeed in their studies.

Revelation: The Importance of Collective Action for Black Women Undertaking Doctoral Studies

Sistas, I have learned a few lessons on this journey. Most of all I have expanded my family. DIVAS are my fictive kin and as such, my membership in this group is one of the highlights of my emerging academic career. Most of all, I am proud to be their friend, sista, othermother, and leader. As I close this chapter, I rejoice in the roadblock and subsequent victories that Toni and I experienced together. She completed her doctorate a year after I did. She is the courage! I leave you with these words to help you in the crossing:

Manage Resistance and Purpose: It is important to note that the doctoral process requires a strong sense of self and an understanding of your purpose. Additionally, in understanding your purpose, you *must* also manage resistance in the academy. There will be many days when you say, "I cannot do this anymore." It is during these days that you envision and revision your purpose. Never undertake a doctoral degree for extrinsic rewards, such as making more money. This will not help you manage resistance. What helped me was the vision of my mother rejoicing in the audience as I walked across that stage to receive my doctorate. When resistance came, I visualized her face, her sacrifice, her love, and unrelenting belief that I could do it. Her face and those of my community in Jamaica and abroad provided a strength that allowed me to overcome. So, in managing resistance and purpose, who can you visualize?

Rejuvenation and Restoration: Throughout the process, find a place, a group, or avenue that will allow you to exhale. The DIVAS collective provides a place of rejuvenation and restoration for Black women to lament, share their victories, and rehearse future success. In an academy or even a program where you might be the only person of color, the impetus is yours to build connections inside and outside of the academy. Annual conferences are great avenues for connection with other Black women in the academy.

Practice Collaboration, Collectivity, and Consciousness: The Jamaican National Motto states "Out of Many, One People." As a Jamaican, I have lived by that phrase from very early. For socially conscious Black women on the doctoral journey, never forget to practice collaboration. You have a responsibility to the collective to build solidarity with other Black women and allies. Being conscious of the collectivist nature of many African-descended communities is essential if we are to build and survive in academic spaces that are foundationally individualistic, Eurocentric, and competitive. Collaboration, collectivity, and consciousness allow for cross-pollination of ideas and actions, freedom from hegemonic constraints, and the creation of a counter-story allowing Black women to articulate our own meaning of self-definition and self-evaluation, examine the intersected nature of oppression, and redefine culture (Collins, 1986). I conclude this narrative with Patricia Hill Collins's (1986) thoughts in mind that

> Black women have long occupied marginal position in academic settings. I argue that many Black female intellectuals have made creative use of their marginality—their "outsider within" status—to produce Black feminist thought that reflects a special standpoint on self, family, and society. (p. 14)

The DIVAS collective represents that "outsider within" perspective. We are a peer-to-peer mentoring, persistence, social, and academic model that other Black women can utilize for success. Create your own DIVAS collective, stand in the gap, academically intercede, and we will begin to change the face of academia forever. I bid you solidarity and Godspeed, my sistas!

2. *Putting on the Garment of Theory: Now You See Me, Now You Don't*

CYNTHIA BROOKS WOOTEN

I now know that experience comes to us for a purpose, and if we follow the guidance of the spirit within us, we will probably find that the purpose is a good one.
— *Ruby Bridges*

Unlike Ruby Bridges going off to school for the first time, the decision to pursue a terminal degree was a pretty uneventful decision for me. I did not have federal marshals escorting me, there was no renowned artist around to capture my walk into the brick-and-mortar establishment, and there was no story about my encounter; that is, until now. However, what Ruby and I did have in common was a support group standing by our side as we embarked upon the educational journey ahead.

I was born in the late 1950s and attended segregated schools in the South, following the Supreme Court decision that outlawed racial segregation in public schools all over the United States. This decision was viewed by many people, my parents included, as a principal leap towards creating a just nation, reflecting the principles on which it was founded (Harris, 1956). North Carolina's answer to this mandate was the Pearsall Plan (Thuesen, 2006), which had the aim of achieving two goals: the preservation of public education in North Carolina and peace throughout North Carolina. Although I hail from forward-thinking parents, I am unsure if my supportive family ever dreamed I would strive for and earn a PhD.

My family has always stressed the importance of education and schooling as the great equalizer. When my parents spoke of "getting a good education," college completion was probably not part of their thinking, mainly because of the financial burden it would have placed on our family's budget. As for my teachers, I am not sure if they even considered higher education as a viable option for me either, as I was one of five children of working-class parents. My perception is based on the seeming absence of attention given to me by teachers, compared to the attention given to other students who descended from parents with college backgrounds and/or had social status in the community. According to Fallon (1997), counselors and teachers may not recognize some students as college material and consequently not encourage them to take part in activities that prepare them for college. Unlike some of my high-school classmates, I was never asked to meet with the school's counselors to discuss my future plans. I concluded that an academic future beyond high school was something teachers were neither recommending nor advocating for me. I perceived myself to be an invisible student.

Therefore, "Putting on the Garment of Theory" explains my Ruby Bridges experience to education, using a framework referred to as "transformative narrative" (Hyater-Adams, 2010). This approach, similar to autoethnography and scholarly personal narratives, emerges from real and imagined visual, written, and spoken stories that become material to use for self-awareness, meaning making, insight, and visioning. Thus this narrative encompasses relevant memoirs of my early years, attending segregated schools in the South, receiving and successfully using my teaching credentials, and later wanting more for my students and myself; thus I returned to college in pursuit of my doctoral degree in teacher education. Yet it details my struggle as a practitioner stepping into a theoretical space where the garment became cumbersome and foreign for the seemingly invisible student.

Through this story, I will paint a visual of my struggles as a first-generation college student (FGCS) with a limited understanding of the college culture (Billson & Terry, 1981) and how my early struggles reappeared in my doctoral pursuit. Hyater-Adams's (2010) research identifies the struggles in my story that create real and imagined visuals and make this a transformative narrative. In addition to my struggle, I later encountered a "family" who did have the PhD goal in mind for me. At this point, my transformation continues. The DIVAS (Distinguished, Intellectual, Virtuous, Academic Sistas) collective was formed in the last year of earning my doctorate, and it could not have been a more opportune time for me. The DIVAS' support lived up to their motto that "Not one will be lost," and I can admit that at times on the journey, I did feel lost.

The neighborhood where I grew up was alive with proletarians. In the immediate surroundings lived only one college graduate (an English teacher). Yet, these parents simply wanted their children, the next generation, to aspire to be better (financially and academically) and attain more wealth than they had. Though my family was always supportive, my grandparents were my true education support system. They were the "kinkeepers" (Rosenthal, 1985) of the family, and always stayed abreast of my academic progress. They desired, communicated, and encouraged an educational destiny for me. Educational memories of my paternal grandmother's hope and wishes are memorialized in two ways. Cherlin and Furstenberg (1986) characterize the behavior of grandmothers as one of imparting a sense of self-worth, participatory, achievement oriented, and persuasive. I saw these characteristics embodied in my grandmother as she encouraged our schooling. Every year we received from her a gift of a 500-sheet pack of notebook paper, two unsharpened number-two pencils, and fruits, nuts, and candy. The school supplies were passed out first, which was not exciting to my siblings and me, but now I realize the gift distribution order was important because education was a priority. Second, my grandmother's bookshelf also carried a sense of importance for our formal learning, and I am certain the books on the shelves were the discards of the people who resided in the homes she cleaned, and I doubt she could even read them herself. Nevertheless, she proudly displayed these books as a reminder to us of the importance of education. These memories are the inner linings of my garment of theory.

I entered grade school not long after the 1954 *Brown vs. Board of Education* landmark decision acknowledging laws creating separate public schools for Black and White students to be illegal; however, schools in my city were still segregated. Though we lived in a predominantly White neighborhood, as my mother prepared to send my older brother to first grade she registered him at the Colored school. The local chapter of the National Association for the Advancement of Colored People (NAACP) was informed of this action, and contacted my parents to enroll him in the White neighborhood school. The NAACP stressed to my parents that optimal education would be the ticket to equality for us educationally, or in the words of Astronaut Neil Armstrong, "one small step for man [my family], one giant leap for mankind [for racial equality in the United States]." My parents followed through and I entered first grade there a year later. The only other people of color at our school were the custodians, Mollie and Mr. Michael (pseudonyms), who adopted us as their surrogates. Mollie treated us like we were her very own, as she was always interested in what I had to say. In a school where I looked different from everyone, she was the first to treat me as if I was not invisible and her concern and support nurtured me. This form of *othermothering* (Guiffrida, 2005) reassured my parents that someone was standing in the gap for their children, as DIVAS stood with me many years later. Othermothering is a central component in the academic and social support structure of DIVAS.

As the othermother, DIVAS made me visible and viable. I was required by my committee chair to engage in a mock dissertation defense, complete with a PowerPoint presentation of my research study. DIVA Sistas attended this mock defense and provided constructive feedback and asked tough questions that I had not anticipated. Some of the DIVAS' questions resembled those asked by committee members in the actual defense. The garment that I had often doubted began to feel as though it was intended for me.

Looking back on my elementary days, some memories have faded, such as recalling my teacher beyond the fact that she was White. Even her name has escaped my memory. I really don't even recall her ever talking to me, but I don't remember her being indifferent to me, either. I may have been invisible to her, or was it that she had not been prepared to teach students like me? After all, this teacher was a White, middle-class female. Was she operating from a sociocultural-conscious perspective? Was she aware of the fact that my experiences were impacted by my race (Villegas & Lucas, 2007)? Although this invisible relationship did not seem to label me as an academic outcast, perhaps being overlooked established a passive disposition in me that I did not realize, possibly viewing this as my Johari Window (Luft & Ingham, 1955), a place evident to others, but hidden from my own vantage point.

My academic memory of the White school recalls classroom time dedicated to literacy instruction. I clearly remember always being in the low reading group, designed for struggling readers. This is where my garment became unstitched. From first through third grade I was a Brown Bird (the notorious label that identified the group for struggling readers). Was this the reason I was not important to my teacher and invisible to all excluding Mollie? Was I invisible because of a cultural capital (Bourdieu, 1977) mismatch? Maybe my teachers were validated in overlooking the brown girl who was a Brown Bird. However, I became a Blue Bird (proficient reader) when our family moved across town during my third grade year and I attended a segregated Black school. The lessons and assignments I experienced were merely reviews of previous teachings and I seemed to be the expert on many things. My new teacher, who looked like me, seemed to be very interested in what I had learned from my previous school. She would call on me often to share my experiences, and somehow I became a "visible" expert in the classroom. This garment was a much more comfortable fit. It felt better being on this side of the "educational track." This is the same feeling I received once I joined DIVAS and began the intellectual dialogues that prepped and strengthened my academic discourse. As we shared articles, insight, and relevant information pertaining to one another's research, we all became empowered through our socialization and social uplift (Guiffrida, 2005).

Many years later, as a successful high school graduate, I was preparing to embark upon a journey that had not been trodden by any previous member of my family. I empathize with Alexandra Duran, who said, "Walking into college as a first-generation student feels like walking alone and blindfolded in foreign territory ..." (Duran, n.d., para. 1). My educational development continued to unfold as I decided to pursue higher education. In the spring of 1978, I went off to college to pursue my undergraduate degree, car packed with minimal essentials and my mind packed with thoughts of conquering the world. I took with me the Ecclesiastes 3:1 passage, "To everything there is a season, and a time to every purpose under the heaven." The season had come for me to enter college and become a teacher, one who would recognize and validate all students from all backgrounds. My goal was to have no invisible students in my class. Incidentally, this goal is probably my deepest connection with the DIVAS—I was visible and important to someone on my educational journey. The DIVAS collective was not only a support system for me, but one in which I provided support for others. All DIVAS have their particular strengths. This mentor-mentee symbiotic relationship with DIVAS kept me in balance with what I needed as well as what I was able to give.

As a FGCS, research predicted the strong likelihood of my failure, as I was a statistic vulnerable to academic (Terenzini, Pascarella, & Blimling, 1996) and social disparities (Martinez, Sher, Krull, & Wood, 2009). According to Smith (2008), the mere fact of my socioeconomic status implied reduced access and the unlikely probability of me even attending college. Research also implied that if I was able to attend college, the odds of obtaining a degree were not in my favor (Howard & Levine, 2004). But I was attending a historically Black college/university (HBCU), a post–Civil War school established to serve Blacks. That is where my academic success emerged, with professors who cared and who also looked like me. After the Civil War, reformers envisioned a place for Colored students to be educated, as they were not permitted to attend other schools of higher education because of Jim Crow Laws (Bullock, 1967). Surely I would be successful here, as I agreed with Du Bois (1935), who said, "had it not been for the Negro schools and colleges, the Negro would to all intents and purposes, have been driven back to slavery" (p. 335). This was othermothering at its best, and it made attending this HBCU rewarding for me.

For once, I felt my voice was heard and my ideas were accepted. I wore my new FGCS robe with comfort and pride. This nurturing style of education prepared me for a successful teaching career, with the arduous tasks of managing a classroom that produced positive learning outcomes for students. Despite the findings of FGCS research, I had the fortitude to work at the college level; therefore, I engaged in learning that impacted my academic performance (Naumann, Bandalos, & Gutkin, 2003). This is contrary to Riehl's (1994) research, which states that FGCSs tend to be less confident about their academic performance.

Although challenging, I was confident in my learning; I persevered and earned my bachelor's degree. Immediately following undergraduate school, at the urging of professors, and prior to joining DIVAS, I applied to graduate school at this same HBCU—Wow, educators who believed in me! This was a first. The professors in my master's program rallied around me to ensure my success. Following graduate school, I returned home and became a second-grade teacher in a Title I school. My career was in its infancy as I was assigned a classroom complete with 20-plus young minds to nurture. Theory, practice, and creativity was used to impact the learning of my students. Although a novice teacher, I felt I was helping my students reach new levels of life and learning, just as DIVAS would stand in the gap and help me reach a new level of learning years later. With DIVA nurturing I was able to step into the garment of theory as they provided a space where a practitioner, such as myself, was given the skills and strategies to personalize theory.

This success propelled me to return to the university classroom as a student. Could I now handle this without the garment that exposed me as a FGCS? A colleague and I decided to make this a partnership. We enrolled in a PhD program together at a local predominately White institution (PWI), arranging our schedules so we could take several courses together, while continuing to work as elementary school teachers. The doctoral pursuit changed my life tremendously, though not like I anticipated. I remember arriving early for my first class, entering the room to take a seat up front. Of the 20 students present, four were Black. Following the formal introductions and the description of class expectations, the professor began lecturing. I began writing profusely. The more the professor lectured, the more I drowned in a sea of academic confusion. My beautifully stitched robe began to unravel in some places. I felt clueless and too ashamed to ask for clarification in front of my peers where I was one of the few older students of color in the class. After all, it was apparent from their participation that they understood the content. My apprehension of verbal engagement, defined by Steele and Aronson (1995) as "stereotype threat," explained my cultural discomfort. I simultaneously wrestled with thoughts of excitement and inferiority related to my doctoral journey. Would this terminal degree be just that, fatal to my professional and mortal existence? My mind wandered to where I would be academically had I remained a low-soaring Brown Bird among a group of students mirroring this class, only years later. This was only the beginning of my journey; one I wish I could say became less treacherous.

Expectations and learning far exceeded my current knowledge. I was entering a culture where the academic language used was not linked to my schema. This was where being a FGCS had its greatest negative impact on me. I wanted to understand information being presented; but with an important missing link, making connections was next to impossible.

With so many years of academic success, I now felt like a Brown Bird again as the theory garment was consuming me. I had been an excellent practitioner implementing best practices, but I now realized I was unfamiliar with their theoretical connections. Needless to say, in order to understand what was happening in the classroom, where I was once again the student, hours of extra reading replaced sleep. My life belonged to my studies. Academic attainment at this level brought new challenges. Consequently and rightly so, I was clueless regarding the scholarly "nuts and bolts" at this level.

Guiffrida (2005) put emphasis on interconnectedness in the othermothering framework. I was missing that link and it felt as though it was an important one. The information I was teaching, and doing a good job at teaching, was not enough to get me through in understanding the theoretical components of my education.

Putting on the garment of theory represents for me the transformation I encountered as I moved from an accomplished educator to a research neophyte, and later to an expert scholar. Research indicated that academically, Black women matriculating at the doctoral level and the likelihood of them earning the terminal degree was now a new set of odds against me. DIVAS became a collaborative network for me on this new journey.

The regular meeting of the DIVAS collective where we engaged in discussions helped me to understand that I was competent to work at this level. One of our founders, DIVA Cherrel, possessed a keen understanding of theory and would many times take the lead in explaining various frameworks. Given that understanding theory was not my strength, I leaned on DIVA Cherrel as a resource. My research analysis and subsequent writing of chapters proved that I was on the right path; my DIVA sistas offered to read and reread my work, and my ability to validate my reasoning and answer their thorough questions confirmed my sometimes doubted ability and self-worth on this journey.

For the first time as an adult I felt academically inadequate, even though I had successfully completed three post-secondary degrees. This is when DIVAS stepped in to be my "makeshift Mollie." I had Black academic women at all levels of the doctoral process to offer support, ideas, and academic advice. When I was unsure, a DIVA sister had the experience and knowledge to offer me assistance. I was making progress at a PWI using DIVA experts just as I was once the expert coming from my predominantly White elementary setting. I recalled my Ecclesiastes 3:1 scripture, "To everything there is a season, and a time to every purpose under the heaven" and knew I was in a new season of my journey with women who looked like and truly cared for me. This is essential to the social and spiritual component of the DIVAS framework, supporting one another in times of need.

According to research (Bair & Haworth, 1999; Fordon, 1996), women matriculating in doctoral programs sometimes may take a longer time to complete their program of study and they may even drop out. Dropping out was not an option, even though as a graduate student I felt isolated. Jacqueline Fleming's (1984) research suggests that Black women are generally found to be the most isolated (academically invisible) group of students on predominantly White campuses. The DIVAS collective and the support I encountered helped me to navigate this doctoral journey to a point where I was able to understand all that had been foreign to me in this world of academia. However, I had to endure troubling situations as I progressed through my studies.

One thing I concluded early on was that my successful completion of the program depended upon the immediate development of a plan and a support system. Research reveals that the act of relating with professors yields a support network that enables students to persevere in their academic pursuits (Tinto, Russo, & Stephanie, 1994). For me, DIVAS was my support network that intervened and encouraged me along the journey, helping me to become more confident about my studies. Empowerment is one of the DIVAS' essential components. I was empowered by the collaboration and encouragement. Again, DIVAS to my academic rescue!

I spent time thinking about why I was having trouble before realizing what was actually occurring was my lack of prior knowledge/background. As an educator, I understood prior knowledge as the information students have that is used in learning new information (Dewey, 1938; Kolb, 1984; Piaget, 1970; Schallert, 1982). This knowledge is commonly considered by Stevens (1980) as "what one already knows about a subject" (p. 151). Biemans, Deel, and Simons's (2001) explanation of background knowledge is "all knowledge learners have when entering a learning environment that is potentially relevant for acquiring new knowledge" (p. 6). As a practitioner, I understood that students who lacked adequate prior knowledge would struggle with learning (Strangman, Hall, & Meyer, 2004) as this knowledge had a great influence on performance (Dochy, Segers, & Buehl, 1999). What was revealing to me was coming to grips with the fact that I lacked the necessary prior knowledge for success in the academy.

My assessment of the dilemma was simple—the need to increase my knowledge of content was imperative for contributions to class discussions. The research was right in front of me, which acknowledged that individuals with familiarity of a topic tend to have better recall and as such are better able to elaborate on features of a topic than those who have acquired limited knowledge of the topic (Chiesi, Spilich, & Voss, 1979; Echevarria, Vogt, & Short, 2008; Vogt, 2005). DIVAS assisted with expanding my knowledge base. As we discussed articles, theories, and research, my comfort level with scholarly dialogue finally became evident. DIVAS saw my potential, and the comfort I felt in my "DIVA garb" helped to establish in me the self-confidence I lacked from my early years. Thus DIVAS developed another doctoral candidate, one who was ready for the academic challenges ahead.

Though seemingly simple, even selecting a research topic was confusing. As a doctoral student, I thought I should focus my research on an unfamiliar topic; hence, I selected literacy. As a practitioner, I was known for the strength and creativity in my math and science lessons; therefore, my dissertation topic probably should have been in the area of math or science. My lack of knowledge about selecting a topic resulted in me living with this decision for my remaining semesters or possibly delaying my graduation.

Though I endured many challenges, rays of light appeared during my data collection as teacher interviews were conducted in elementary classrooms. My frequent classroom observations took me back to the times when I was the expert—a foreign feeling since this journey began. This task also helped to bring clarity to the mounds of literature woven into my methodology chapter. As a result, my research conversation became evident in scholarly dialogues and my once awkwardly fitting "garment of theory" now drapes me comfortably. Currently, as an assistant professor in an all-women's HBCU, I share my well-sewn garment of experiences, courage, passion, and dedication with each teacher candidate whom I prepare, so that she will never experience the "invisibility" that hid me and my potential.

Epilogue

So, who should care about an FGCS who grew up attending segregated schools and became an accomplished teacher and PhD candidate? This story should serve as a confirmation of the fact that by overcoming and persevering life's obstacles one can accomplish far beyond what is imagined. Though every journey on this road is different, if my story inspires but one to pursue a PhD, then I have won the battle. For those scholars, I leave the following words of encouragement with you, some of which come from the wisdom

I shared with my biological children as well as tips as suggested by Green (2008).

Stay poised and confident. Allow your passion to be your voice and do not let others deter you or persuade you differently. Had I listened to the research that stated my family would not have the means for my post-secondary education or that I would not graduate from college, I would not be where I am today. I sincerely believe that if my road led to me earning my PhD, then your road too will yield the same success. I encourage my DIVA sistas by saying, "Begin this PhD journey with the end in mind, and remember, let no one define you by telling you this journey is not for you!"

Persevere until you reach your mark. Though there may be struggles along the way, continue to do whatever it takes to help you reach your goal. As I struggled to find the right educational fit, I continued to forge ahead. My road started with my makeshift Mollie and ended with DIVAS: note the timespan of my perseverance.

Establish relationships to enhance your skill set with your professors. Pairing with professors to work on projects better prepared me for my actual collection of data. While working as a volunteer on such projects, I learned how to prepare data for interpretation. My advice is not to be afraid to initiate this action; approach your professors and offer your services.

Establish relationships with peers within your program. For me it was beneficial to network with the individuals within the department (such as DIVAS). Engaging in scholarly discourse with peers is less intimidating and is powerful in gaining an understanding of perspectives/interpretations of others.

When things become difficult, take a break and reward yourself. For me this meant putting everything down and treating myself to an ice-cream cone. A sabbatical period is recommended to rejuvenate one's mind during the process.

Taking everything into account, if you are passionate about what you are doing, you can make it. Just remember, "Life comes with many challenges. The ones that should not scare us are the ones we can take on and take control of" (Jolie, 2013, para. 18).

3. Collaboration and Encouragement as Mile Markers: Running for the Prize of PhD

CYNTHIA THRASHER SHAMBERGER

Strength to Run
Who put me here to run this race?
Where does my help come from?
How can I take another step to endure this journey's strenuous pace?
I look to the Great Creator within and find the strength to run.
The open window lets rain on my face, no sleep all night long.
Trying to stay awake to meet a deadline, hating the country
music whine, as I drive along. Exhausted in this difficult space—will I ever get done?
Looking to the Great Creator, again, I find more strength to run.
Lonely days and lonely nights, tears and groans and sighs are
mingled with those who care for me, cheering from the sides.
Until at last the journey's done, the victor's prize is won.
Now I lift my voice, my eyes, my hands and thank
The Great Creator within for being my strength to run.
— Cynthia Thrasher Shamberger

As I contemplated what lay ahead, the sun rose and chased away the morning dew, revealing the beauty of our surroundings and its intricate details. Like taunting bullies, competing voices in our heads made us doubt whether we could finish the half-marathon race. Although we live in separate towns, my daughter and I managed to train by encouraging each other via email, phone, and text messages. I also travelled an hour one way, so we could train together whenever possible. The half-marathon experience with my daughter parallels my interactions with the DIVAS (Distinguished, Intellectual, Virtuous, Academic Sistas) on many levels. The race in the mountains was long and painful at times, and we were absolutely the last two to finish the 13.1 miles.

But together we did it—we finished! The half-marathon medal now hangs in my home office on the wall opposite where my PhD degree is beautifully framed and mounted. Each award is a testament to what can be accomplished through the power of collaboration, support, and encouragement from a caring community of family. It was my biological family member who helped me earn a marathon medal, and my DIVAS family who supported my academic journey.

Deciding to Run

My entrance into public education was as a lateral entry (temporary emergency license) teacher in special education. Despite my general love for interacting with people and what I consider a calling to work with youth, I was angered at the lack of respect shown by some of my fellow teachers and administrators towards often disenfranchised families with children who identify as having one or more disabilities. Awareness that African American students in special education classes have been overrepresented for decades (Sanders, 2012; Scott, 2013) prompted my desire to help teachers become more skilled at facilitating better outcomes for all students. This includes students who receive special education services—including correctly identifying students with special needs, working to reduce inappropriate referrals, supporting struggling students in the general classroom setting, and working with culturally and linguistically diverse families, especially those having children with disabilities. I believe that positive professional relationships within the school setting are foundational to improved student outcomes (Friend & Cook, 2013). Additionally, I share Foster's (1993) view, gleaned from the Committee on Policy for Racial Justice (1989), that connectedness among school, families, and communities is equally important, if not more so (in my case), for students with disabilities. In Foster's (1993) discussion of the education crisis seen by the African American community regarding their children, she explains a dissonance between traditional reform research and a few studies by notable Black scholars (Committee on Policy for Racial Justice, 1989) who find that traditional school-reform policy recommendations are

> ... unresponsive to the needs of the black American community and fail to recognize the centrality of human relationships in the teaching-learning transaction. They [notable Black scholars] contend that "African-American children are not likely to excel unless they and their parents can feel a sense of connection and identification with the school and the school personnel assigned to serve them. (p. 102)

In order to keep my teaching job, I returned to school to obtain a teaching license. During those years of commuting more than an hour to attend classes and completing online assignments whenever I could, I continued teaching, and my dissatisfaction with the school environment for students with disabilities increased. I left that school at the end of the academic year and shortly thereafter accepted a position in a neighboring district. Changing to a new school in a different county was a personal improvement, but just as in the former location, the students' educational experience was not optimal. This was due partially to ineffective communication among general and special education teachers, parents, and school administrators. This realization sparked a desire in me to work towards improving school outcomes for students with disabilities by helping the adults involved work together more effectively. Thus, after obtaining teacher licensure, I went on to earn a master's degree in special education. It was then that I began thinking and praying about pursuing a doctoral degree so I could have greater influence in preparing special educators, as well as their general education counterparts and administrators, to work collaboratively for the sake of all children. My reasons for leaving the classroom were similar to those suggested by Carter (2002) who found that many women of color in special education pursued higher education as a means to help students and their communities. As a result, when a funding opportunity became available for me to pursue a doctorate, I decided to run the long distance race to earning a PhD. I examined my strengths, weaknesses, resources, and motivations in order to assess my potential for completing the journey. In reality, I hardly knew what lay ahead and soon found myself struggling with the rigor of the program and stumbling along the way in loneliness as one of a few Black women, and older than most other students. I was roughly halfway through my doctoral program when I joined the DIVAS and received the help that I needed.

Unlike the academic settings of my former special education students, the doctoral program was a generally positive experience. Moreover, the DIVAS provided critical elements to my experience that were missing. This chapter tells of my journey toward earning a PhD and the wonderful support system that encouraged me along the way. An integral part of this story includes a network of sharp Black women, the DIVAS, who invited me to join them on an inspiring, collaborative journey of similar pursuit and who saw me through to the completion of my degree. Joining them was like becoming a member in a running club after running alone for a long while. The team environment was inspirational. This collective exemplified what Guiffrida (2005) and Foster (1993) described as "othermothering"—a critical factor needed for addressing the academic and social well-being of school children that can also be extended as a viable means of helping Black women doctoral students become degree completers.

Running the Race and Enjoying the Journey

At the time that I began my program, the shortage of university faculty in the field of special education had reached a critical point, making recruitment of solid graduate students interested in becoming faculty members a high priority (Cartledge, Gardner, & Tillman, 1995; Montrosse & Young, 2012). Likewise, the department made it a priority to provide its doctoral students with numerous resources and experiences designed to help them successfully complete their programs. In reflection, my department held to several of Steele's (1997) "wise schooling" tenets designed to support all students, but of most value to Black female scholars. These resources included supportive advising, faculty mentoring/coaching, opportunities to co-author articles for publication with faculty, internships, projects with peers, and opportunities to present individually or in groups at state, national, and international conferences. Researchers agree that these are some meaningful ways to support minority doctoral candidates (Felder & Baker, 2013; Washburn-Moses, 2007). These experiences gave me exposure to real-world dealings in the field of special education and they were excellent in adding value to my learning during the doctoral process (Gasman, Gerstl-Pepin, Anderson-Thompkins, Rasheed, & Hathaway, 2004). Although these practices outlined by Steele (1997) were generally present in my department in varying degrees, I still felt a longing and a need for something more but could not quite articulate what that something was. Looking back, this feeling was similar to what bell hooks (1990) describes as a yearning that fills the heart with a desire to give and receive knowledge in multiple ways. I needed knowledge that would enhance my daily life on the PhD journey and strengthen my capacity to survive the process (hooks, 1990).

More specifically, despite the enjoyment, success, and support from my spouse, family, friends, and the department, I often felt isolated, burdened, inadequate, exhausted, frustrated, and stressed out (Thomas & Hollenshead, 2001). These areas of struggle often seemed to be rooted in a sense of fear that I was not cut out for this endeavor and would not be able to finish my degree (Taylor & Anthony, 2000). In regard to feelings of not belonging, Simmonds (1992) posits that "it is our otherness as Black people *and* as women which means that we have to connect and link aspects of our lives to others" (p. 57). Upon further reflection of Steele's (1997) "wise schooling" paradigm, three other factors are identified as equally important to program completion: regular affirmation of being intelligent enough to belong in the academy; continually expressing the value of my perspectives; and providing role models of other Black women scholars at various stages of their programs in particular, and their social, emotional, and spiritual lives in general (Patton, 2009). Fries-Britt and Turner Kelly (2005) confirm that these were the pieces missing from my experience as a Black female scholar, which came into focus once I joined the DIVAS. It was not until I became part of this collaborative collective of Black female scholars that I realized that in order to stay motivated and make progress in my program, I needed the vision, wisdom, knowledge, skills, and encouragement shared within a community of other likeminded Black women in similar situations (Merriweather Hunn, 2008; Patton & Harper, 2003). Thinking of novice runners, they initially experience the rigors of various levels of training to enhance their fitness and performance, but then they begin to experience a "runner's high." Similarly, with the DIVAS I began to experience new levels of support and encouragement. It was then that I actually began to enjoy the journey.

Collaboration: Leaving the Familiar Path, Running New Trails

Historically, collaboration, especially in education settings, has been difficult to investigate and encapsulate into theory. Thus, it lacks a clear, widely accepted definition that spans across—or even within—disciplines (Cook & Friend, 1991; Gajda, 2004). Although it has been a topic that has gained increased attention over the past several decades, confusion over a specific definition makes it imperative to describe what constitutes collaboration—and what does not. Gajda (2004) argues that many people erroneously assume that any activity carried out with another person or group is collaboration. Others authors have contributed various perspectives across disciplines to the discussion of collaboration (Bronstein & Abramson, 2003; D'Amour, Ferrada-Videla, San Martin Rodriguez, & Beaulieu, 2005; Huxham & Vangen, 2000). A definition of collaboration offered by Cook and Friend (2010) explains that "collaboration is the style professionals select to employ based on mutual goals; parity; shared responsibility for key decisions; shared accountability for outcomes; shared resources; and the development of trust, respect, and a sense of community" (p. 3).

These authors also emphasize that collaboration in the true sense of the word can only exist in certain conditions. For interactions to be characterized as collaborative, group members must (a) come to the table voluntarily as equals, (b) exercise parity (equal power in decision making), (c) embrace mutual goals, (d) share resources, and (e) share responsibility for all out-comes. They further clarify that several additional factors are prerequisite to the initiation of and sustainability of the collaborative process. These include how members value collaboration, believe that their collective work has a greater potential to result in desired outcomes than if they work individually, and the practice of that belief over time becomes the lifeline of the group.

This definition of collaboration was the foundation of my graduate work and it intersects with the mission and goals of the DIVAS. The main points of intersectionality are the bolts (as they are referred to in the introduction) of voluntary and fluid membership, spiritual and social connections, and the valuing of collaboration over competition. Group members accept that life circumstances may prevent participation in some group meetings and activities. Members also ask for and offer prayers for each other in monthly meetings and in other forms of communication on a regular basis. Further, it is the expectation that we all collaborate with and celebrate each other rather than work alone. Just as trail running can be an exciting and challenging departure from other types of races, joining the DIVAS has compelled me to leave the familiar path of isolation, along with my own thoughts and perceptions, to explore new trails of opportunity for personal development and group ac-complishment within the collective (Fries-Britt & Turner Kelly, 2005; Hub-bell & Burman, 2006; Paulus & Nijstad, 2003).

Othermothering and Mile Markers: Navigating the Course

The DIVAS introduced me to the concept of othermothering, the centu-ries-old tradition of supporting a nonrelative child like a family member (Guiffrida, 2005). This concept was demonstrated in our collective through multiple pathways that include commitments to each other to advise, men-tor, be a role model, push together toward full academic potential, provide consistent support and advocacy, and be a collective source for personal and emotional counseling. As doctoral students (and one recent graduate in the beginning), the DIVAS fluidly gave and received advice from each other, en-gaged in problem solving, and shared career networking tips. We often car-ried each other's social, emotional, and spiritual burdens, and collaborated on community service activities.

Particularly inviting to me was the opportunity to make meaningful connections with other female scholars who looked like me, and the com-ponents of the DIVAS framework made that possible. For example, mem-bership in the group was voluntary and fluid; thus, when someone could not attend meetings, notification was usually sent. Having a two-hour round-trip commute to regular meetings left me struggling with whether to attend any given meeting. But the draw of the sisterhood and their encouragement always won me over. Participating in a mentoring relationship was mutually fulfilling as I poured into my mentee, and she in turn inspired me (Patton, 2009). Since my mentee (referred to as a "DIVA Sis") and I attend the same church, it was relatively easy to check in with each other before or after church services, although we scheduled other times to go out for a meal or visit in her home overnight. At other times, phone calls, texts, and emails sufficed. I introduced this young woman to the DIVAS and made it my mission to push her toward her full potential, specifically within the collective and in life in general. Connections with other women have ebbed and flowed as needs arose. Opportunities presented themselves for me to mentor other DIVAS, especially for spiritual encouragement and emotional support. For example, I shared discussions with single women struggling with the demands of their program and their desires for marriage and family. Other women helped me by sharing tips on organization—an area in which I struggled. Our mentoring experiences mirror those described in Patton's (2009) qualitative study of mentoring experiences among African American women in graduate and professional schools. Women in the study believed that access to Black women mentor relationships was very important although difficult to attain. A similar study by Woods (2001) echoed the difficulty Black women scholars face in trying to establish successful mentoring relationships. Additionally, research by Jackson, Kite, and Branscombe (1996) found that African American women in graduate programs sought out mentors who "looked like" them and who took them under their wings—and even into their homes—in order to promote retention and persistence in their program of study.

Especially uplifting were the testimonies of the good things that happened in the lives of the DIVAS whenever we gathered. It was common for emails to "fly" and "light up" the inbox with good news. Equally important were communications to provide prayer support and words of encouragement when a DIVAS member faced difficult circumstances. Scholars agree that it is imperative to support the spirituality of doctoral students in order to help them achieve their PhD goal (Okpalaoka & Dillard, 2011). All of these things combined—the hugs, prayers, testimonies, collaboration, retreats, holiday socials, annual DIVAS conference planning, and resource sharing (I received a special donation for my trip to Kenya)—serve as mile markers that keep leading me back to the DIVAS. Within the collective, the intersectionality of collaboration and othermothering occurs within the space of shared goals, every voice valued, an organic environment of mutual trust and accountability for the success of the collective (Fries-Britt & Turner Kelly, 2005; Gasman et al.,

2004; Guiffrida, 2005). Williams (2004) supports this type of mentoring as a motivating factor in doctoral degree completion among African American graduate students, stating:

> This tribal or communal behavior, which is almost instinctive, communicates an allegiance that ensures mutual success. If one student has access to beneficial resources, he or she openly shares them with the others. If one student struggles or fails, the whole group grieves for that individual… . In this setting, there is a consistent, unwavering commitment to the success of the group. (p. 241)

The above quote represents in part what Williams (2004) describes as a collectivist mindset, which places higher value on the learning community rather than on individual accomplishment. Similarly, through othermothering and peer mentoring, the DIVAS celebrate individual accomplishments along the way toward the common goal of PhD completion. Despite the fact that when I joined the DIVAS the concept of othermothering within the academy was new to me, it became like a welcome drink of cool water on the long, tedious journey toward my degree.

Potholes and Hurdles

When deciding whether or not to pursue a doctoral degree, and occasionally as a member after becoming one of the original DIVAS, I faced enormous fears that had the potential to be stumbling blocks on the road to my PhD. The biggest one was fear of possibly losing or severely compromising my marriage. This fear was born out of a little book that I had read years before the PhD opportunity. It featured highlights from interviews of 32 successful African American women with doctoral degrees in various fields, including higher education. The majority of the women self-reported as being divorced, single, or separated (Ehrhart-Morrison, 1997). At the time, I had been married for about 30 years. Yet, without having details of these women's situations, I began to fear that if I earned a doctoral degree I might lose my spouse in the process. Brock (2005) exposes the hurt, pain, and life-shattering experiences that divorce can bring, which for some can eventually become life-defining.

Researchers have identified several factors that may impede Black women scholars' progress in PhD programs. These may include having to balance the demands of various relationships with family, friends, and community with household chores, cooking, cleaning, and other responsibilities along with the rigors of graduate studies (Carlson, 2001; Stohs, 2000). Similarly, Besharov and West (2002) have also argued that Black women scholars often face an intense struggle by the dueling priorities of career and family.

Gasman, Hirschfeld, and Vultaggio (2008) use socialization theory to describe difficulties faced in graduate programs by Black doctoral students. These researchers examine student needs through social connections and interactions that are initiated and maintained outside of departments and the academy, as well as the lack of social connections and interactions within the academy. However, strategies found to be critical to the success of Black women in doctoral programs include finding strength in God, family, friends, and the community—to whom they also want to give back (Patterson, 2006). These same strategies have been employed within the DIVAS collective. I kept my marriage a top priority, which resulted in continued support for my endeavors from my husband. Admittedly challenging at times during my program, I enjoyed married life and considered my spouse my closest friend (and still do). However, other worries such as finances, maintaining social and extended family interactions, leisure activities, church involvement, and whether I was actually capable of such an endeavor were just as burdensome. Thus, I was anxious about possible difficulties that could arise as a result of my involvement in the academy (Patterson, 2006). These fears would often appear suddenly, like holes in the road, but my faith, husband, and support network, which included the DIVAS, helped me along the way.

Run for the Prize. Cross Over. Repeat

An ever-present feeling of anxiety seems to permeate the lives of doctoral students, especially black female PhD students (Watt, 2003). To combat the high level of stress in my own life, I began to take regular walks around campus. It was an inexpensive pleasure with multiple benefits and was much needed due to the sedentary nature of my program. I always felt better after a walk. Sometimes I would even jog for three to five seconds—that's all I could manage at first. However, over several months I worked up to participating in a 5K run/walk in December of my second year. It was during this time that I began to equate the long process of earning my PhD as a journey, much like a long-distance footrace. Both are processes that depend not only on the skill and dedication of the individual, but for me also on the encouragement from faith, family, friends, and support networks like the DIVAS.

Shortly after completing that first 5K (where my son ran his first half marathon at the same event), my daughter and I decided to spend about four months training for a half marathon in the North Carolina Mountains. Then, at dawn one Saturday morning in June 2009, we set out on our journey, which was mostly downhill. However, 13.1 miles is still a long, difficult feat to accomplish—even if it is downhill. It was during our months of training and subsequent participation in the half marathon that I began to notice a recurring theme in my doctoral experience that I was struggling to develop. The emergent theme of persistence (or rather my lack of it), along with the patience to endure my preparation threatened to interrupt or end my journey. Researchers including Holmes, Land, and Hinton-Hudson (2007) have documented the struggles that women of color experience on the road to attaining the PhD and attest that "the journey to higher education for many Black women has been long and arduous" (p. 106). But just like I prayed and pushed through to victory in the half marathon with the encouragement of my daughter/race partner and our spouses, a new and different kind of encouragement arrived. I soon discovered that in the DIVAS, a treasure had been found along this long, arduous journey to the PhD.

In retrospect, what the DIVAS offered is what I had been missing. For example, intricately intertwined into my doctoral experience were spaces that my doctoral program minimally addressed (if at all). These included needing a greater sense of connectedness expressed not only through collaborative activities but also through expression of my Christian faith. Watt (2003) discusses ways that African American women graduate students cope with the numerous difficulties associated with program rigor, socioeconomic status, and racial and gender oppression. Institutions are challenged to strive for a more holistic and student-focused approach to meeting needs that are common to most doctoral students as well as those that are particularly unique to African American women doctoral students (Gasman et al., 2004).

The construct of othermothering (Foster, 1993; Guiffrida, 2005) is foundational to the framework the DIVAS collective is built upon. Collaboration as a style of interaction is often practiced by DIVAS as each one helps another to realize their goal of program completion. DIVAS embody both theories to ensure the needs of Black women are addressed in order to help Black women maximize their doctoral experience and realize their full potential. Living at the intersection of othermothering and the concept of collaboration makes the DIVAS a thriving entity where Black female scholars are supported to completion of their doctoral programs, through job searching, and induction into faculty or administrative positions in the academy. This collective of Black women scholars epitomizes the powerful dynamic of relationships built on collaboration and community to promote shared excellence (Foster, 1993). I have witnessed and experienced this within our network of mutually supportive doctoral students and newly minted junior faculty. The collaborative endeavors and sharing of community we have engaged in to help each other through our programs has been challenging yet inspiring. In her book *Sista Talk*, Brock (2005) reiterated Collins's (1989) perspective that knowledge for Black women scholars is best developed not in isolation, but rather in dialogues of safe communities. As such, DIVAS has been a valuable part of what each of us needed to complete our programs and then reach out to help others still in the PhD pipeline, and our experiences herein will be treasured for multiplied lifetimes.

Running in Circles

I needed this group. Although my department was supportive, this group provided a deeper sense of belonging and a higher degree of sustained collaborative effort (Williams, 2004). Being an older married student with adult children close in age to some of my academic peers did not make me stand out in a negative way. Rather, I came to feel like an older sibling in a big family, who, as a commuting student, happened to live out of town instead of across town. Every time I pressed my way to our monthly meeting, I was glad I had made the trip. Often, because many of us share similar spiritual values, I left feeling encouraged and motivated to keep going.

The group also provided professional development in abundance, through practice of presentations, giving and receiving feedback on writing, and offering tips on interactions with faculty and job search information. Opportunities to co-present at conferences were regular occurrences. Supportive interactions were not limited to the academy but also involved home, community, church, hobbies, and holidays shared with family and friends. Social and emotional support during family celebrations and crises was the norm. In her study of eight Black women doctoral students, Patterson (2006) described the complex roles, interactions, expectations, and obligations that can simultaneously be supportive of and taxing on progress towards degree completion. Examples include caring for elderly family and/or community members who provide encouragement and (older) children who can help out with household chores but also require attention and support in their schooling and activities. The DIVAS remained member centered by constantly seeking input on what we needed corporately and individually to complete our degrees (Gasman et al., 2004). Responses led us to bring in speakers, form small groups of like interests and needs, listen to and critique each other's presentations, and read each other's draft manuscripts, etc. For me personally, it was tremendously encouraging to participate in the monthly meetings, share my struggles, and hear someone else's struggles, or praise reports of accomplishments or milestones. In addition, the firm and loving leadership of my spouse, who insisted I take occasional well-deserved breaks from my studies (even though my laptop was often an unwelcomed but necessary guest) was invaluable. Conversely, I often offered support and wisdom from my expertise and experience to others within the group. One of the greatest motivating activities we experienced was attending each other's doctoral defenses and graduations. By far, the most gratifying experience for me has been earning my PhD in August 2010 and then starting my first faculty position a day later!

Now, as a Dr. DIVA, I am still running with the other sistas who need me. I am following in the footsteps of our founders, Dr. Cherrel Miller Dyce and Dr. Toni Milton Williams, and I am circling around to othermother Black female scholars still in the PhD pipeline to ensure that they too receive strength to run and complete their journeys.

Questions to Consider

As you consider whether to pursue a doctoral degree, the following are questions to keep in mind:

1. What research are you interested in to the extent that you would do it with no reward in sight? This is important because there may be times when you feel like giving up due to the inevitable hurdles that arise. Examples include racism in many forms, lack of respect or understanding by family and friends or fellow academicians. Additionally, you might experience an inability to draw boundaries to enable yourself to attend to the strenuous responsibilities associated with degree completion (Brock, 2005).

2. Why is the PhD important to you? It is important to keep your purpose in focus. Questions 2 and 3 will be considered together since potential answers may overlap. Establishing a purpose for pursuing a doctoral degree is essential to persistence for degree completion. Identifying those whom you need to lean on for support and those whom your work will benefit will also play a major role in your matriculation. Gregory (1999) posits that historically, many Black women seek higher education to better themselves, future generations, and the communities in which they live.

3. Who will your work benefit and how will you keep going when all you want to do is quit? A study by Carter (2002) found that Black women left teaching in special education classrooms in order to provide more help to students with disabilities and their communities. In addition, I want my work to benefit general and special education teachers and their administrators as they support students and families. Patterson's (2006) study described how several Black women doctoral students

credited their relationship with God as their source of strength for enduring the PhD process. For example, church attendance, prayer, and their spirituality were mentioned by participants in the study as key elements to their persistence.

4. Where can you find genuine support and are you willing to apply what you have learned to help initiate a similar group? Patton and Harper (2003) emphasize the need for Black women doctoral students to have networks for mentoring and support both inside and beyond the academy. These might include faculty and/or peer mentors, or other individuals from among family, friends, and the community with knowledge of the academy.

Lessons for the Future

There are two main things to take away from this chapter. The first is that Black women scholars don't have to matriculate through their doctoral programs in isolation and frustration. The second is that prospective doctoral candidates need to be made aware of the many ways that marriage and other relationships could be affected during the doctoral process. There is a great need for establishing communities of learning that also take into account social and cultural needs. When Black women doctoral students commit to the hard work of collaborative interactions and the practice of othermothering, then each person within the group has the opportunity to gain the rewards of engaging in mutual support. Thus, more Black women scholars can realize the prize of earning a doctoral degree.

4. Black Wonder Woman: Demystifying the "Supernatural" Powers of the Black Female Doctoral Student

CHERYLL SIBLEY-ALBOLD

Calling all Sistas (A DIVAS Love Poem)

Come, come, come, run, run, run, I to you will come and run
Calling, calling, calling you, oh sister, my sister run ... hurry, please come
You're falling, falling and we are calling ... calling out to you ...
Above their lies, please hear our cries ... didn't they say
Black is not beautiful? LIE,
Afrocentric is not scholarly? LIE
Sister my sister don't you understand?
Those are false ideologies to keep you under their command
Negative self-esteem implanted when they stole us from our native land
As a people we've been falling, falling, so sister, my sister, listen
DIVAS is calling ... calling to you ... and this is our decree
Collective hands are outstretched to catch you, loose those chains of self-doubt
Don't be afraid to set your intellect free ... oh sister, my sister, you can lean on me
When you're not strong ... and convinced you won't make it to the end.
My sister, my friend ... A safe place awaits in the warm embrace of your DIVA
sisters.

Like the heroine Diana Prince of the 1970s hit TV show *Wonder Woman*, which I grew up watching during my most formative years (yes, I know she was played by a Caucasian actress, but stay with me), I am a superhero. I am the progeny of West Indian Amazons—a legacy of Black wonder women analogous to the Amazonian all-female inhabitants on the fictional "Paradise Island" depicted on that show. I too am from an island and just like Diana Prince I learned many supernatural things from my mother, grandmother, and later my DIVA sisters, all incredible Black women who possessed great energy and fierce determination. These women defied objectification, and moreover, used their intellect and great inner strength to overcome adversity. They are my superheroes, each and every one.

In this chapter, I share my own early experiences with race, gender, and ethnic identity as an immigrant child in America and in particular, how the intersectionalities of these social constructions of personal identification influenced my motivation and self-beliefs before and during doctoral study. First, I briefly discuss how the influx of Black immigrants in the U.S. over the last three decades is changing the dynamics of what it means to be Black in America and the composition of the Black student population on America's most elite campuses. Next, I integrate concepts adapted from the perceptual psychological theory of "perceived affordances" (Gibson, 1977) as an alternative lens through which to contextualize how a salient and positive Black Caribbean immigrant ethnic identity, wherein education achievement has been integral to the successful higher educational attainment of this generalized ethnic group, may actually serve to promote the development of a positive academic self-concept (Mitchell, 2005) and influence beliefs about personal agency (Bandura, 2001).

Most important, is that I reflect on my own experiences as a Black immigrant woman pursuing the PhD degree. Therefore, I describe my own unique perceived affordance that I euphemistically label conditioning to become a "Black Wonder Woman." Using the phrase "Black Wonder Woman" as a metaphor, I hope to illustrate how early on the matriarchal role models in my life and later my membership in DIVAS conditioned in me innate survival instincts, inner strength, and abilities to successfully balance multiple roles while navigating the doctoral degree. I articulate how this particular perceived affordance has deep historical, gender, ethnic, and cultural origins. In my experience a natural artifact of this in-group connectedness (Oyserman, Harrison, & Bybee, 2001) is that it is a major source of pride, accountability, and responsibility that has empowered Black immigrants' notable transgression of deficit-model academic stereotyping and racial minority stigmatization in U.S. higher education.

Similarly, the DIVAS collective is a counter-narrative to deficit-model discourses regarding all women of color seeking the PhD degree and decries Black women relating in opposition and competition with each other for the limited positions in the academy. DIVAS, by our mission, rejects the "lone wolf" ideology that historically pervades the pursuit of the PhD. DIVAS could best be described as an academic family where we are proud, accountable, and responsible to each other. Thus for me, becoming a founding member of DIVAS was organic to my nature, as I viewed the sisterhood as an opportunity to be a part of another group of Amazonian women. Guiffrida (2005) captured our essence in that we go "above and beyond" for each other when we provide "comprehensive advising regarding career guidance, academic issues, and personal problems" (p. 708). In DIVAS, we found a communal place for authentic communication about the experiences of Black women in academe.

Finally, I share several adaptive strategies, including a longitudinally enduring connection with DIVAS, that helped me to complete my PhD degree in compressed time (two and a half years from coursework to dissertation defense) while balancing the concurrent life stresses of my multiple roles as wife and mother.

Coming to America

Immigration represents a significant portion of the increase in the U.S. population and estimates of the total numbers of U.S. immigrants were at one time around 34 million people or 12% of the total population (Keller & Tillman, 2008; Kent, 2007). U.S. immigration in the early 1900s was predominantly that of European ethnic groups. However, beginning in the early part of the 21st century, European-descent immigration percentages dropped drastically from 92% during 1900 until 1909 to a reported low of 16% in 2005 (Vickerman, 2007). As a result of the implementation of the U.S. Diversity Visa program, which relaxed entry requirements in the early 1990s, the greatest numbers of immigrants since then have been reported to come from Asia, Latin America, Africa, and the Caribbean (Benson, 2006; Foner, 2001; Kent, 2007; Vickerman, 2007).

Prior to 1965, estimates were that 90% of the U.S. Black population were the descendants of American slaves, or native Blacks (Rong & Brown, 2002). However, in just over a ten-year period from 1990 through 2000, two immigrant Black groups, Africans and Caribbeans, were estimated to be responsible for 25% of the growth of the U.S. Black population (Kent, 2007). After the 1990s, the two largest foreign-born Black groups in the U.S. were Caribbeans and Africans. Collectively, the literature refers to persons of African Caribbean and continental African birth, parental ancestry, or descent as "Black immigrants" (Benson, 2006; Kent, 2007). In 2005, the number of Black immigrants tripled from 1980, when over one million Black children born in that year were of African or Caribbean immigrant origin, a status granted if their parentage included at least one parent who was foreign born (Kent, 2007). It is important to note that the term "Black immigrant" is an umbrella term and therefore is very limited in capability to detail the great geographic and cultural diversity that comprises both the Caribbean and

African continent. Nonetheless, I have selected the term to describe myself and my experience.

According to Vickerman (2001), the four sizeable Caribbean Black ethnic groups in the U.S. are Jamaican, Guyanese, Trinidadian, and Barbadian immigrants, also known as Anglophone Caribbeans (Foner, 2001). The rapid influx of Anglophone Caribbean emigrants from their native islands changed the composition of the U.S. Black population, especially in metropolitan centers like New York, Boston, and Miami (Kasinitz, 2001). As a group, Black immigrants have a complex dual identification, not previously demarcated in American society, in that they often identify themselves as racially Black but ethnically do not identify as African American (Kasinitz, 1992).

Now, several decades later, the first- and second-generation children of foreign-born Blacks are a population of growing numbers and significance in the higher-education system (Barton, 2006; Massey, Mooney, Torres, & Charles, 2007). Between the years of 2000 and 2007, the percentage of Black students attending college has increased steadily from 11.3% to 13.1% (National Center for Educational Statistics, 2012). How many of these students were of immigrant origin? Unfortunately, a major challenge for higher education is that Black immigrants, such as those from the African continent and the Caribbean, are noticeably absent in the statistical data profiling today's Black college students (Keller & Tillman, 2008; Phelps, Taylor, & Gerard, 2001). This oversight persists even though there is statistical evidence of a diversity of ethnic nationalities, other than African Americans, within the Black college-student population (Barton, 2006; Phelps et al., 2001).

> The greatest challenge at present is the changing face of American higher education due to the influx of new populations of students. In parts of the country, people of different nationalities, cultural identities, and races are sharing academic spaces, creating hybrid identities, new languages, and new academic cultures. (Barton, 2006, p. 1)

In their recent study using National Longitudinal Survey data ($N = 1,028$), Massey, Mooney, Torres, and Charles (2007) reported that first- or second-generation immigrant Blacks made up approximately 13% of the U.S. Black population. However, at the 28 higher-education institutions included in their study, 27% of the Black students were from immigrant origin. Overall, they found that the proportions of immigrant Blacks were higher at private institutions and highest at elite colleges, such as the Ivy Leagues, where immigrants made up 41% of the Black student population.

Massey et al. (2007) concluded that at the 28 institutions they studied and dissimilar to other ethnic groups, such as Latinos and Asians on campus, immigrant Black college students were disproportionately overrepresented on these campuses relative to their ratio in the Black population. Moreover, the difference in GPA between White students and immigrant Black students was less than the difference between the native Black students and White students at these selective colleges. In a related finding, Roach (2005) reported that two-thirds of Harvard's 2003–2004 academic year Black students' parents were African and Caribbean immigrants.

Intersectionality of Race and Ethnicity

My earliest and most enduring memory of being an immigrant in America, at the tender age of 10, was being told that I was not Black. The first to inform me were the African American children in my elementary school, who told me I was not Black because I spoke differently, ate the wrong foods, and was in their exact words "born in a banana boat." The White children told me I was not Black because I didn't live in the housing projects. Instead of ridiculing my birthplace, the island of Jamaica, they referred to it as a tropical paradise and even more surprising, some had happily vacationed there with their parents.

From these early and contrasting childhood conversations, I quickly learned that the Western vernacular used to categorize and describe people in American pluralistic society lacked the sophistication demanded for the complexities of identity, especially in regards to ethnic and cultural ascriptions. This is evident in that many Americans often use the terms "race" and "ethnicity" interchangeably (Benson, 2006). For example, it is common in American lexicon to use the terminologies of "Black" and "African American" interchangeably and even synonymously. It is especially problematic in the racial identity literature, where authors often conflate race with ethnicity, and neglect or disregard national origin or nativity (Benson, 2006). So it was not surprising that for the Black children I encountered when I first came to the U.S., to be Black in America was to have an African American experience.

Perception Is Everything

Gibson's (1977) famous work on the ecology of perception posited the concept of objects possessing what he called "affordances" or perceived and actual properties that influence their utility and interfaces with the contextual environment. Gibson further describes affordance and non-affordance as invisible or visible, known or unknown, desirable or undesirable relationships between a person and the world regardless of an individual's ability to perceive them.

Appropriating this theory to the topic of this chapter, I offer this concept here as an alternate lens for elucidating how a strong ethnic in-group connection (Oyserman et al., 2001) with my Caribbean heritage and matriarchal foundation, unbeknownst to me, fostered my resilience to endure the academic rigor of doctoral study and fuelled my persistence in obtaining a terminal degree. It has been argued that socialization in predominately Black contexts external to the United States may serve as a protective factor against the negative stereotypes associated with being Black in America (Glick & Hohman-Marriott, 2007; Ogbu & Simons, 1998). This alternate frame of reference and pride in ethnic identity over physical manifestations of race may indeed offer a unique albeit invisible affordance, one that may provide Black immigrants with a different set of intangible racism-deflecting strategies based on perceived and actual cultural affordances with which to moderate U.S. negative educational stereotypes of minorities (Glick & Hohman-Marriott, 2007; Vickerman, 2001). My major premise is that Black immigrants cultivate and pass on this affordance to their children to aid them in navigation of our unique social dichotomy; we have a dual identity—first, a camouflaged ethnic status as immigrants, and second, extremely high racial visibility as Blacks in America (Foner, 2001; Kasinitz, 2001; Kent, 2007; Vickerman, 2007).

Overriding the stereotypes that negatively depict minority populations in the U.S. has historically proved to be difficult (Oyserman et al., 2001; Steele, 1997). However, early on my parents instilled in me a deep sense of pride for my origins, Jamaica, West Indies, a place where Black skin was in the majority. According to Vickerman (2001), "'Blackness' is normal in the West Indies in the way that Whiteness is normal in the United States" (p. 241). Thus, as I grew older, I also grew increasingly proud that I was a child of Black and moreover Jamaican immigrants. I believe that as a protective measure my parents purposefully taught me to identify racially as Black, but regard myself as a Caribbean ethnic person. They reinforced my ethnic identity through food and storytelling. Thus, I was raised to steadfastly identify with my ethnicity over my race, a strategic distinction in a race-conscious country such as the U.S.

My parents conditioned in me a social and cultural connection to being ethnically Jamaican over the physical color of my skin. Immigrant groups place greater salience on ethnic identity as their in-group characteristics. They have been known to segment themselves in order to maintain their cultural values (Kasinitz, 1992; Vickerman, 2007). More specifically, Vickerman (2007) noted that immigrant Blacks have a "relatively complex conceptualization of race compared to the United States; and an immigrant mentality that downplays race in favor of achievement to validate the decision to migrate" (p. 156).

Over time, my self-esteem and self-concept strengthened based on this perceived ethnic affordance and it influenced the way that I chose to view my learning environment and eventually the development of my positive academic self-concept (Mitchell, 2005). Therefore, I posit that this was an immigrant-origin affordance that affected my interactions with my environment and disposition towards what I could achieve academically and greatly contributed to my development of a positive academic self-concept (Mitchell, 2005). Essentially, I was raised to believe that I could achieve anything through a powerful combination of two immigrant work-ethic ingredients: self-determination and higher education. Therefore, when I encountered negative stereotypes in the American education system developed to stigmatize and threaten the self-concept of Black students (Steele, 1997), I did not internalize them as relevant to my lived experience. I believed that as long as I worked hard and applied myself my teachers would reward my efforts—and they did.

Johnetta B. Cole (1997) said, "who you are is about where you've come from and where you are going" (p. xx). Some argue that Black immigrants, as a collectively identified group, may develop alternative perspectives about racial and ethnic identity and self-concepts due to their majority position in their homelands and voluntary status in the U.S. (Ogbu & Simons, 1998). When I was growing up as a young Jamaican immigrant child in America, my parents routinely invoked the frame of reference that they were voluntary immigrants. Coming to America was a deliberate choice they made. Repeatedly, they told me that the sole purpose for emigrating was to provide me access to a better education. So it was my responsibility to acquire the best education that would give future generations of my family access to a better life and achieve more than past generations.

Intrinsically, this has always fueled my motivation for high educational attainments. I truly believed that many Black immigrant parents strategically deploy this ethnic culture uplift message to empower their children to resist deficit thinking, and thus prevent them from becoming a victim of America's Black or White race dichotomy. In her poem "Still I Rise," Maya Angelou powerfully states, "I am the dream and hope of the slave." Throughout my childhood, I heard that my academic and professional accomplishments resulted from the sacrifices made by my parents leaving their native land and the dreams of proud, defiant Caribbean slaves, and also those of millions of hope-seeking Black Caribbean immigrants in America. I grew up watching Jamaican families work tirelessly for their dreams in America and yes, often in multiple jobs. Thus, I credit a large part of my success and persistence during doctoral study to the matriarchs of my family, an enduring West Indian and Caribbean immigrant legacy steeped in obstinate self-determination and an abiding faith in education for generational and ethnic group uplift.

It was with such deep conditioning and unique ethnic cultural affordances that I walked away from a lucrative job in the Southwest and enrolled in a PhD program in the South. From the beginning, I felt confident, strong, competent, and capable. I resolved to complete my degree with the same efficiency that I had seen in my matriarchal role models. I would become an academic scholar while continuing to care for my family and nurture my marriage in the process.

My Caribbean ethnic foundation afforded me with what I later realized was a strong self-concept and a highly developed sense of personal agency (Bandura, 1997; Pajares & Schunk, 2005). This must have been a visible trait because at various times while pursuing the PhD, my DIVA sisters and I were asked "how do we do it" by our White (mostly childless) classmates because of our seemingly remarkable abilities to multitask, our resilience in the face of setbacks and challenges, and most of all our perseverance. They appeared genuinely baffled by the fact that we prioritized our families and valued equally our multiple roles as wives and mothers, in addition to emerging academic scholars. Some observed that our academic role models, female professors in the institution, chose scholar careers over childrearing, sacrificing one or the other but rarely being successful at both. In fact, the implication was that trying to have a commitment to a family might make us less credible as academics.

Intersectionality of Racism and Sexism

As Black women, we have the ironic status of having to be strong in a society that historically sanctioned the perception that women were supposed to be the weaker sex. I would argue that as Black women, we developed our strength because we were not afforded the opportunity to be weak. As far back as 1851, Sojourner Truth eloquently articulated the marginalization and dichotomous experiences of Black women in American society, when she asked the paradoxical question

> And ain't I a woman? Look at me! Look at my arm! I have ploughed and planted, and gathered into barns, and no man could head me! And ain't I a woman? I could work as much and eat as much as a man—when I could get it—and bear the lash as well! And ain't I a woman? I have borne thirteen children, and seen most all sold off to slavery, and when I cried out with my mother's grief, none but Jesus heard me! And ain't I a woman? (para. 2)

Of course we are women, with similar needs as our Caucasian counterparts. Concomitantly, just because we resiliently juggle and struggle, often without complaint, we should not be made out to be a mutation of our sex. In *Sista Talk*, goddess Oshun emphatically states of Black women that "We have been taking care of our families, our men, our churches, and our communities since even before Ida B. Wells worked to end lynching" (Brock, 2005, p. 27). Throughout history, Black women have done amazing things and of course we do not really have supernatural powers, and it is important that as Black women we not try to be superwomen. Superwomen stand alone. For Black women, I believe the exact opposite is true. When we come together, across the Diaspora as in the case of DIVAS, we unmask to reveal our vulnerabilities, our fears, and draw strength from each other. We are instead wonder women, because it is when we identify with each other and help each other that we become empowered.

I want to point out that the fictional television character Wonder Woman not only did not wear a mask, she also did not actually have any special powers; instead she had the right tools (bullet-deflecting bracelets, a shield and a lasso) at her disposal and the history of her people—she harnessed the power of a group of women and most of all their collective intellect to defeat her challengers. In DIVAS, our deep coalition is our most powerful tool, which beyond support, gave us real resources and tacit knowledge to succeed (Guiffrida, 2005). In truth, for many our individual degree goals became more attainable once we began helping each other.

In this regard, I want all women of color, regardless of ethnicity, to know that they too are Wonder Women. For the women in my family, the women of the African Diaspora, and especially my fellow DIVAS, I am eternally grateful. I am the full beneficiary of their hard work and they have passed down to me a rich legacy of gender-based strategies and cultural weapons to navigate, balance, and persevere. We are Black women. We worked laboriously and tirelessly raising families and pursuing our academic and professional goals. Our marriages and our children can flourish no matter what we choose to do for ourselves. It was simple; I could do no less for my family than what my mother and ancestors did for their families. It is all that I know—an affordance as a result of the intersectionalities of my ethnic heritage, gender, culture, and race.

Parting Advice

As a result of reading this chapter, I hope that contemporary Black women and especially Black immigrant and definitely Caribbean women considering the path to the PhD will affirm that they are capable, competent, and possess the inner strength to complete this journey. The best advice is to not do it alone. Through DIVAS, we were able to express our frustrations, share accomplishments and concerns, invoke the healing power of laughter, and set goals and develop plans. In DIVAS, we quickly realized that as aspiring Black female academics, our individual successes were intertwined. You cannot fail if in your lives strong Black women through history and family legacy remain "the edifice for your own consciousness" (Brock, 2005, p. 28). I am who I am because of my mother, my grandmothers, and a long legacy of Black matriarchs. Patricia Hill Collins (2003) states our ultimate non-affordance: "Black women cannot afford to be fools of any type, for our objectification as the Other denies us the protections that white skin, maleness, and wealth confer" (p. 55). In closing, I recommend the following DIVAS strategies for successful and efficient completion of a doctoral degree.

Claim your victory before you begin. Immediately after being accepted into my doctoral program, I wrote my name as Dr. Cheryll Sibley-Albold on a small sheet of paper and I tucked it way. In times of frustration, I would retrieve it, and looking at it in print always helped to motivate me over the next hurdle.

Dedicate it to someone important or inspirational in your life. My degree was always a personal goal, but it was also a promise I made to my father as a little girl and it was a tribute to all the matriarchs in my family history.

Navigate and take control of your journey. Remember you are the chief operating officer of your degree. Believe that you can do this. It is a misconception to believe that you are not in control, but to be effective you must understand the culture of the PhD and utilize the appropriate hierarchies. Demonstrate humility for the process, respect your advisor and committee members' expertise, and exhibit personal commitment and accountability.

Make it a priority. You must dedicate unencumbered time to this. Let go of what is not important. Remove yourself from all distractions, especially when you are in the writing stages. I devoted almost every single Saturday for almost a year to writing my dissertation. I barely watched television for more than three years!

Chart your progress frequently. Know and research all the courses, requirements, and major steps (e.g., coursework, comprehensive exams, proposal, and dissertation). Develop a degree timeline that can help you organize and track every step and related tasks to completing your program.

Focus and narrow your interests. Pick a passionate topic early, and expect that it will change. Refine it constantly but keep it simple and achievable.

Do research before the dissertation. Take advantage of opportunities to work on any kind of research in any capacity to master the concepts prior to your own dissertation project.

Get connected early. Do not do this alone; find at least one other person with whom to compare notes and share experiences. Groups like the DIVAS are important for sharing information, networking with persons at different stages of the PhD process, and most importantly celebrating each other's progress. In groups you are able to validate one another's positive or negative experiences.

5. *Invisible Woman: A DIVA Seizing Visibility*

Toni Milton Williams

Without light I am not only invisible, but formless as well; and to be unaware of one's form is to live a death. I myself, after existing some twenty years, did not become alive until I discovered my invisibility.

— *Ralph Ellison*

I was sitting on my front porch enjoying the warmth of the mid-morning sun massaging my arms and legs while I was on the phone with Cherrel, a fellow doctoral student who had recently completed her PhD. While we spoke I was reminded of the nightmare and degradation that I had experienced as a Black woman in the academy. Nonetheless, I utilized this experience to navigate my way through the completion of my doctoral program. Cherrel and I were dissecting my comprehensive exam experience. The comprehensive exam is one of many capstones in the doctoral process. It is a written and oral examination required of all doctoral students who have completed coursework with the next step resulting in designing a pilot study. I had to retake the oral exam because I had failed. I was left defeated and feeling as though I did not belong in the (White) academy. I felt invisible.

Up to this point in my academic career, I negotiated and enacted identities with which I was not always comfortable. Glenn (2012) recounts, "we often receive conflicting messages from varying sources about who we are, who we are becoming and who we should be" (p. 133). There were times when I felt I had to represent and defend the Black community, and because of that I became invisible to myself and had forgotten about the giants whose shoulders I stood upon. Although I was accepted into the doctoral program, I quickly understood that being accepted was the easy part and that the process and the work had just begun. Audre Lorde (2007) asserts, "if I didn't define myself for myself, I would be crunched into other people's fantasies for me and eaten alive" (p. 137). I was embarking on the Black woman graduate experience, one that involves and requires resiliency, strength, courage, support, and perseverance. I was ready to define myself.

I felt lonely and infuriated because I lacked the implicit knowledge not given to Black women in the academy. My ability to use scholarly language to verbally explain my written answers as a novice Black woman scholar was in its early stages and I needed more practice. I entered a culture in which I wanted to succeed, but I was not explicitly taught the ways of thinking and knowing, the ways of negotiating power and status, nor was I provided with the resources that I expected to get at this level. Engaging in dialogue for teachers, scholars, and critical thinkers is a means of crossing boundaries that may or may not be erected by differences (hooks, 1994). The conversation reached a pivotal moment when Cherrel and I realized that other Black women at that particular university may have stories similar to mine and that those stories and feelings needed to be shared with one another in order to persist and succeed in the academy. "As Black women, it is imperative to construct environments of support and opportunities for professional development that are mutually beneficial" (Fries-Britt & Turner Kelly, 2005, p. 5); hence the DIVAS—Distinguished, Intellectual, Virtuous, Academic Sistas—collective was established. DIVAS became an impetus for me to explore the identities I carry as I ponder how my life has spoken to me in various contexts and how I came to be who I am today (Holland, Skinner, Lachiocotte, & Cain, 1998).

This narrative describes those identities not only as a part of a story of perseverance, courage, and inner strength, but also as a part of my realization that the invisibility I felt as a doctoral student could be contradicted. It describes empowerment through remembering the teachings of my childhood community and recognizing the support of mentors—doctoral sisters, professors, and the distant teachers who write the books and articles that I read. Through this process, I have been able to move beyond the invisibility I felt after my comprehensive exams to find freedom and mobility as a Black woman scholar. My story demonstrates the significance of a supportive academic community while attaining a doctorate and adjusting to the dynamics of academia. My narrative is part of a mosaic of other Black women who provided me with professional support, encouragement, and a sisterhood as I pursued my doctorate, thereby offering context to historical and cultural events of people of color (Dixson & Rousseau, 2005). The process of writing this story has taught me that I have multiple and competing identities with which to contend, including wife, mother, educator, and researcher, which make my existence as a Black woman in the academy one that can be both empowering and oppressive. Beverly Tatum (1997) explains my entangled thoughts:

> The concept of identity is a complex one, shaped by individual characteristics, family dynamics, historical factors, and social and political contexts. Who am I? The answer depends in large part on who the world around me says I am. Who do my parents say I am? Who do my peers say I am? What message is reflected back to me in the faces and voices of my teachers, my neighbors, store clerks? What do I learn from the media about myself? How am I represented in the cultural images around me? Or am I missing from the picture altogether? (p. 18)

With these thoughts in mind, this narrative explores events, people, and experiences that had an impact on my identity from my early undergraduate school days, through my comprehensive examination, to the development of DIVAS and the influence of distant mentors, and back to the community of my childhood.

Removing Blinders: From Undergraduate to Graduate School

Completing my undergraduate degree from a small predominately White all-women's college (also known as a predominately White institution, or PWI), was an experience that afforded me with opportunities to become personal with my professors and examine my identity as a young Black woman in a setting largely reserved for White females. Holland et al. (1998) contend that "Identity is a concept that figuratively combines the intimate or personal world with the collective space of cultural forms and social relations" (p. 5). There was no support organization such as DIVAS in place during that time so I learned to reach out to peers, professors, and staff members to create a community of support.

I found my passion and my place at the small all-women's PWI through acting, as it provided me the space to explore diversity of identity through portraying various characters. Deconstructing characters in order to portray them on stage allowed me to examine my multiple identities in that environment. In short, I had to learn about who I was in order to be true to the character I was playing and I soon realized that my identity was based on social contexts and interactions (Tatum, 1997). I was appointed as the stage manager instead of a cast member for one production and was terribly disappointed. Soon after finding out the news, I was invited to a friend's room for a photo shoot to portray campus life for recruitment at the college. More blinders were removed weeks later when I looked anxiously at the final product and saw myself as the Other; a Black female, eating pizza, having fun, and laughing with her White friends during a study break.

After this incident, not wanting to be seen as the Other, I began to rene-gotiate my role in this environment as I searched to define my identity as a Black woman while obtaining an undergraduate degree. I found myself other-mothered by a Black staff member who greeted me with a smile and encour-agement on a daily basis. She made herself available to talk to me and to listen to my frustrations as well as share her own at times. My social identity was beginning to flourish in the context of my interactions with those around me (Harris & González, 2012). However, the power I gained through my social identity was quickly taken from me in my statistics class, one that was particu-larly strenuous for me. During class, I needed further explanation of a problem and asked the professor to clarify the concept for me. His curt reply humiliated me. Essentially, he responded that he did not think I was adequately prepared for class and didn't seem capable of doing the work. Words and actions that exemplify unconscious and subtle forms of racism are called racial microag-gresions (Pierce, 1974; Solórzano, Ceja, & Yosso, 2000). In that moment he had stolen from me the confidence that I needed to excel in that class. Ra-cial microaggressions in both academic and social spaces have consequences, which leave African American students struggling with feelings of self-doubt and frustration as well as isolation (Solórzano et al., 2000). His statement silenced and stripped me of my dignity as an individual and as a young Black woman. As Dewey (1997) asserts, "any experience is mis-educative that has the effect of arresting or distorting the growth of further experience" (p. 26). In this sense, I was left feeling ashamed and humiliated for asking about a con-cept and had been clearly reminded of my position in that class as yet another blindfold had been removed.

In my doctoral studies, I was enrolled in a course titled "African Amer-icans and Education" and was told by my White female professor that I was "very integrated" once I shared that Good Homes, the neighborhood in which I grew up, was the first all-Black community in my hometown. I also shared that my K–12 experiences were shaped by the exposure to White culture and values because my classmates and teachers were predominately White. My initial thoughts were, "What do you mean? I'm *very* Black!" My aunts fought for civil rights in Alabama and are still hometown heroes in Montgomery today. How could my professor make that assumption? Perhaps it is because she witnessed the way in which I had assimilated to the European way of doing school and as Tatum (1997) recounts, "the aspect of identity that is the target of other's attention, and subsequently of our own, often is that which sets us apart as exceptional or 'other' in their eyes" (p. 11). Being told I was integrated made me feel as though I had done something wrong, as though I had offended her and perhaps my White classmates. It was as though I was not Black enough. She had just made me visible to *myself.* It was in that moment that I felt empowered and began to dig deeper into my identity as a Black woman, not an integrated one.

Solórzano et al. (2000) contend, "racial microaggressions in both academic and social spaces have real consequences" (p. 11). During that class I shared insight about negotiating being Black in predominately academic and extracurricular settings and what it meant to grow up in an all-Black community, and my professor interpreted my experience and concluded that my Blackness did not matter. Because we constantly modify and communicate our identities in and out of the academy, women of color are frequently in precarious situations as we find our career paths (Glenn, 2012). This denial of my cultural knowledge and skills by my professor was absurd to me. Her comment pushed me to examine my role as a Black woman, student, and educator, and I began to remove the blinders that encapsulated me. Entering the doctoral program drove me to question my intelligence and confidence as a Black woman. Even as I think back on completing my undergraduate degree, I have felt that my voice as a Black woman in the academy has been undervalued because there has been no room for it. In identifying with the Ellison (1952/1995) character, the Invisible Man,

> ... my problem was that I always tried to go in everyone's way but my own. I have also been called one thing and then another while no one really wished to hear what I called myself. So after years of trying to adopt the opinions of others I finally rebelled. I am an invisible [wo]man. (p. 573)

In my rebellion, I seek to find a space for my voice and those of my sisters in the academy.

Defining Myself: The Comprehensive Examination and Beyond

The comprehensive exam is a written and oral examination required of all doctoral students as they complete coursework but prior to designing the research study that will become their dissertation. For me, it was a debacle. I sat at the head of the oblong table with my committee members bombarding me with questions that I could not fully comprehend. I needed time to process the questions but it seemed impossible. I felt as though I was trapped in an academic jail cell with no means of escape, support, or survival. The more my committee spoke, the more I began to shut down and become invisible until finally I was asked to step outside so the committee could deliberate my fate. Time stood still for me in the cold, brown, lonely hallway. Tears swarmed my face as I waited, hoping for a committee member to come and tell me that I had *passed*. I began to think that I would not be worthy of being in the academy (Ladson-Billings, 2005). African American teacher educators often feel a tension Ladson-Billings (2005) compared to slaves who worked *in* the Big House but were not *of* the house. She explains, "they [African American teacher educators] are in the academy but not of the academy. Their roles are circumscribed by race and the social conditions of African Americans in the broader society" (pp. 4–5).

The reality was that at the pit of my innermost soul I *knew* that I had failed my oral exam. I knew that I had mixed up one too many theorists and that my examples were absurd and that I felt oppressed in that moment. I felt powerless because I knew that even if I presented the copious notes I had taken and the way I had organized all five of my color-coded binders for each question, I still could not verbalize and communicate that knowledge. I relived the experience in my head so many times, yet I still could not fully understand what happened. Where had I stumbled? Whose name should I have mentioned that I left out? What should I have clarified in more detail? I was confident and knew the material, and the more I reflected, the more I realized that it was my presentation. My words were jumbled and I lost my focus. It was difficult for me to remember the key researchers in my field and provide relevant examples. Even more, I could not eloquently verbalize my thoughts into a scholarly conversation. I simply choked. I felt a silent disgrace within my department; it was as though I had a badge of infamy sewn across the front of my blazer.

Residing in the academy is both a privilege and a burden. Clearly it is a privilege because of the attendant perquisites, but it is also a burden because it invites a closer, less forgiving examination of one's competence (Ladson-Billings, 2005, p. 8). Upon recounting the entire experience with a colleague, I realized that I needed specific support as an emerging Black woman scholar. I needed support with a cultural foundation. I needed a mentor who understood who I was as a Black woman, wife, mother, doctoral student, and who was willing to guide me as such. I wanted the academic othermother who valued education and could help the education of others (Bernard et al., 2000). I needed the support of an academic family, an othermother, and fictive kin, a sister who understood what I was up against and could show me how to prepare myself for the academic world and the scholarship it demanded. I needed the support of the DIVA network.

I knew that I had to persevere in order to master my second attempt at my oral comprehensive exams. I had to learn a new language and my words had to be carefully crafted. I reminded myself of what I had to do, "Instead, speak with their words only long enough to make your point known in a way that those who hold the 'power' can understand and accept" (Brock, 2005, p. 124). I kept a notebook with me (and still do) to record thoughts and conversations with professors and peers as well as notes on readings for my personal reflection and connections. I scheduled meetings with a committee member who coerced me to elaborate on all of my scholarly thoughts during each session. I also started having car conversations with myself to hear myself speak. Even more, I met with a fellow DIVA sista on a weekly basis to discuss my scholarly reasoning. I no longer sat silent and invisible in presentations at national conferences. I boldly introduced myself to presenters whose work I admired after sessions and eventually was able to extend our conversations over dinner through the years. I began to see myself as a Black woman scholar and I successfully defended my second oral comprehensive exam. hooks (1994) explains, "The academy is not paradise. But learning is a place where paradise can be created" (p. 207). I found my paradise.

Being Seen: DIVAS Begins

It wasn't until that summer day on the phone that Cherrel and I decided to reach out to fellow Black women and their friends in the doctoral program for an informal conversation to meet one another. Our first meeting took place in the library one month after that conversation. Women trickled in by pairs of two and three laughing, hugging, and screaming. Two hours later as the meeting ended in prayer, it was decided that we would continue to meet and mentor one another and I put my trust in a small circle of women who gave me a sense of community and spiritual and emotional uplift.

DIVAS became a place for me to grow and be challenged by my peers without embarrassment. Harris and González (2012) maintain, "women of color must perform their social identities carefully and selectively to avoid being criticized, marginalized, dismissed, or rejected by colleagues and students" (p. 8). The DIVAS provided a space to examine these identities and what they meant to us as collective and individual researchers. I surrounded myself with Black women in the doctoral program with similar experiences in and out of the academy. Additionally, we shared the same goals and disappointments on this unfamiliar path of intellectual evolvement. We mentored one another into the academy. As we referred to one another as "sis" or DIVA, our community was becoming a solid foundation for success.

As a collective, we began to understand the concepts, generalizations, and rules that contextualize the Black woman graduate experience. We maintained monthly meetings, yearly retreats, and co-presented at conferences (supported and provided opportunities to practice the skills that were being cultivated). Moreover, we critiqued one another's scholarship in order to strengthen our academic speech skills. We were living what Fries-Britt and Turner Kelly (2005) write about: "because there are so few faculty of color at PWIs (predominantly white institutions), students of color often look to each other for mentoring" (p. 223). Monthly DIVAS meetings became a place of serenity, empowerment, and approval. The DIVAS bond transcends walks of life and disciplines. The meetings became the place in which I confirmed my identity and I did not have to compromise my ideals or myself. Having an academic family provided me with opportunities to self-regulate and self-evaluate in an affirming way with my sisters who were walking on similar paths. The final piece of my identity comes from the neighborhood in which I grew up, where my personal journey begins, and where I claimed my visibility.

Looking in the Mirror: Reaffirming Childhood Lessons

"Efforts to develop our professional selves often create tension about what it means to be a woman of color because our ideas of identity are influenced by family members, peers and society influence our ideas of identity" (Glenn, 2012, p. 133). Being a part of DIVAS reminded me of my hometown community and the guidance I received as I searched for visibility. Good Homes was the first all-Black community in my town and it was a part of the foundation of my identity, a key element in "nurturing my sense of black heritage" (Ellison, 1952/1995, p. xx). I reaffirmed my cultural foundation by attending and speaking at my childhood neighborhood's 50th reunion. Being taken back to the fact that I grew up in the first all-Black neighborhood in my town helped to renew my self-confidence. I was reminded that I was indeed standing on the shoulders of courageous giants in my community, which included nurses, small-business owners, military servicemen and women, community leaders, and educators. It was during this community function that I was able to honor my individual complexity while reflecting on my cultural identity (Holland et al., 1998). The entire community instilled respect, determination, and perseverance in me, all characteristics that I had to redefine as a doctoral student. Speaking at the event and looking at the smiling, approving faces of the elders of my community reminded me of my purpose, my visibility, and identity. I realized that social identities emerge in the context of interaction (Harris & González, 2012), and that mine began in this community. I am reminded that my presence and voice matter and that I am not alone on this journey.

As a doctoral student I questioned my purpose in the academy and whether it was where I wanted to begin my career. Moving through the program and building a support system that was unique to me was the highlight of my success as a doctoral student. My individualized support came from the DIVAS, peers from other institutions, and self-selected mentors, who included faculty members who were not committee members, those I met at conferences, and members of the community in which I was raised. Gaining visibility throughout my doctoral experience required me to critically examine myself as a Black woman *in* the academy. The DIVAS sisterhood has shaped an awareness of who I am. Failing my comps taught me that I was a Black woman outside of the academy, yet to be *in* it. That experience shaped who I would become as a researcher and a teacher educator. Throughout this journey, the DIVAS have become a source of knowledge and networking. The DIVAS challenged me as I learned to navigate the academy by validating me as a Black scholar, and providing critical feedback.

Parting Thoughts

Having a family while being a full-time doctoral student entailed challenges that included leaving my family to attend conferences for days at a time, sacrificing family time on weekends, and forgoing some holidays in order to read scholarly journals and write my dissertation. Monthly DIVAS meetings became a place of serenity, release, empowerment, and approval. There are DIVAS with similar family situations and the meetings gave me space to express my frustration at having to balance the task of doing it all and being Superwoman. The DIVA bond transcends across walks of life and disciplines. The meetings became the place in which I found my identity and my peace with my academic family.

As you begin your road to the PhD, think about who you are as an individual and connect this person to who you want to be as a scholar. Chart your journey daily, weekly, or monthly. Using a journal or notebook is a great way to record thoughts to reflect and grow from as you persist. Insert power and inspirational quotes and scripture in your journal to encourage yourself. Join organizations in your field and take time to network at conferences. While attending conferences, ask questions in sessions and make contacts for future collaborations. Furthermore, take the opportunity to handpick mentors who are working at other colleges and universities so you will have an outsider's perspective and advice as you navigate the academy. Find accountability partners/peers within various disciplines (DIVAS) who will support you with tough academic love for the times you need transparency. Lastly, find a theme song that will inspire you when you are on the verge of quitting and ignite you as you prepare to orally defend your comprehensive exams, proposal, and dissertation.

Sankofa, the Root of Who I Am

Sankofa is a West African symbol that means "going back to our roots in order to move forward." When I think of roots, I think of family and community; however, I also visualize the roots of a tree or a plant. I am reminded that roots support and absorb in the same way that my family and DIVAS community do. Throughout my journey I am grateful for my weathering roots. They demonstrate the strength and endurance of my ancestors. I have learned that my roots grow wide and deep, and are plentiful. I have secondary roots for extra support. My roots are wild, and grow uncontrollably. I have learned to embrace my roots for who they are, without judgment. After all, they have endured with me all these years. I honor my family history as I tell how I endured and became like the lotus flower that grows in a murky environment. The lotus emerges through the murk and muck to become a beautiful flower; much like me persevering through the academy to bloom into an empowered Black woman scholar.

6. Tales from a Hip-Hop DIVA: One Girl's Journey from the Bronx to the PhD

Dawn Nicole Hicks Tafari

Broken glass everywhere
People pissin' on the stairs, you know they just don't care
I can't take the smell, can't take the noise
Got no money to move out, I guess I got no choice
(Fletcher, Mel, & Robinson, 1982)

I was raised in Edenwald Projects in the Bronx. Edenwald was urine-soaked staircases, shootouts at dusk, and crackheads. It was also "Red Light, Green Light: 1, 2, 3," "Hot Peas and Butter," and hip-hop. I do not miss Edenwald, and I do. It was my culture—one riddled with drug abuse, sexual molestation, and hunger. Hence, I begin this chapter with "The Message" by Grandmaster Flash and the Furious Five. This song speaks to me. It relays the pain and frustration I often felt growing up. "The Message" spoke to my reality (Pride, 2007). And though I resent many of my Edenwald experiences, I respect the role that they have had in my development. For those experiences, coupled with the support of a powerful "village" (family, community members, teachers, friends, hip-hop), made it possible for this Bronx girl to achieve a PhD. Since I was introduced to the Distinguished, Intellectual, Virtuous, Academic Sistas (DIVAS) in 2011, they have come to encompass a large part of my village. The DIVAS is a collective of Black women on both sides of a terminal degree who support one another by offering emotional encouragement, academic assistance, networking opportunities, and friendship. This kind of community proved to not only be necessary for me to maintain my sanity while undergoing the rigors of doctoral study, but the DIVAS Collective is also an essential part of my growth and development as an empowered Black woman academic.

In this chapter, I take you on a voyage through a series of vignettes. The five vignettes work collectively to illustrate five specific moments of impact that helped to shape my journey from the Bronx to the PhD. The first vignette, called "Loving Hip-Hop," is the tale of how I came to recognize myself as a child of hip-hop and member of the hip-hop generation (Kitwana, 2002). The second vignette, "Meeting bell hooks," is about my first experience being othermothered (Guiffrida, 2005; James, 1993) by a complete stranger and how this led to my appreciation for bell hooks (hooks, 1993). The third vignette explores my coming into knowing an Afrocentric feminist epistemology (Collins, 2003) and is called "Knowing Patricia Hill-Collins." "Feeling Joan Morgan" is the fourth vignette, for it illuminates the pleasure I felt when I learned that there was a term to describe who I have been all of my life: a hip-hop feminist (Morgan, 1999). In the last vignette, "Embracing the DIVAS," I share my experience being embraced and cared for by the DIVAS in an othermothering fashion as sisters in academia and in life. Finally, I close this chapter with a few parting words of love for those of you who may see yourself in my story.

Loving Hip-Hop

I am hip-hop. Hip-hop[1] is the culture of "my people"—Black people, people from the inner city, people born between 1965 and 1984 (Kitwana, 2002). My love for hip-hop is deep. I was born in 1974, and hip-hop's music, art, and language are the foundation of everything I know. The first record I ever bought was Salt-N-Pepa's "The Showstoppa" (Azor, 1985). I loved this song because it was a rebuttal to Slick Rick and Doug E. Fresh's "The Show": a tale of how they met and subsequently disrespected a girl. In "The Showstoppa," Salt-N-Pepa respond—ferociously, fiercely, and unapologetically. I felt empowered, and without even knowing it, I was receiving my first lesson in hip-hop feminism[2]: I have a voice—even within this male-dominated culture. I could sense my inner-DIVA Sista blossoming: a woman who would one day find her place amidst an academic world that is validated by white, male, elite voices. In fact, the strength I gained from hip-hop helped me to navigate my reality. I grew up during the crack boom, and many of my friends were either drug dealers, drug dealers' girlfriends, or perpetuating the culture of poverty. Alternatively, I joined a dance group called "Rhythm by Nature," and we performed in amateur and professional venues. Soon after, I began to be cast in hip-hop and reggae music videos. I loved the attention, the semi-celebrity status; moreover, I loved being a part of the culture that I cared about so deeply.

However, hip-hop began to change in the mid-1990s. The expectations of dancers began to change.[3] Simultaneously, I had entered college, began reading bell hooks, and started growing my locs. I began to not be cast in videos as often, and I began to refuse some of the castings I was offered if they required that I wear a type of "attire" that I found unacceptable. Because hip-hop was becoming an internationally lauded and recognized culture, the gaze of corporate America was upon it (Gause, 2008). Corporate exploitation and negative media influence commodified and manipulated hip-hop into something with which I had less and less in common (Gause, 2008; Morgan, 1999). Though hip-hop had saved my life and provided me with an outlet of expression, hip-hop and I were growing apart. I still saw my life in hip-hop's reflection; however, my exposure to the world (especially bell hooks) was changing me.

Meeting bell hooks

I first met bell hooks in the summer after my freshman year of college. A couple of my girlfriends and I were heading home on the 2 train, talking and laughing, when a woman who looked about ten years older than I, approached me and othermothered me (James, 1993). She told me that she had overheard us talking and was wondering if I had ever heard of bell hooks. I told her that I hadn't, and she recommended that I read a powerful book by bell hooks called *Sisters of the Yam.* I had no idea who this strange train woman or bell hooks were, but she'd piqued my interest. I appreciated her othermothering spirit, so I found the book and read it.

As I read the book, I felt enlightened and empowered. I learned that I wasn't the only Black woman who was struggling to develop a positive self-concept. I learned phrases like "white-supremacist capitalist patriarchy" (hooks, 1993, p. 1), and I was pleased to find terms to help me understand the "forced ghettoization" (Ogbu, 2007) and poor educational and socioeconomic conditions that I had experienced (George, 1992). I learned that I could not ignore the intersection of my race and my gender and that a "renewed black liberation struggle can only be successful to the extent that it includes resistance to sexism" (hooks, 1993, p. 3). This knowledge was liberating because it gave me a voice. It helped me to take a stand against the sexism that I had witnessed in hip-hop culture. Furthermore, I learned that "those of us committed to feminist movement, to black liberation struggle, need to work on self-actualization" (hooks, 1993, p. 5). I did not know about the DIVAS at this point in my life; I did not have the guidance and mentoring of likeminded academicians who also looked like me. Yet I realized that I had personal, internal work to do if I wanted to make any contribution to the world. I had spent my freshman year distracted by boys and parties. However, I entered my sophomore year a more focused young woman with a new attitude. bell hooks taught me how to reflect, which set me on the trajectory to not only finish college but also to become an educator, pursue advanced degrees, and to be ready to receive Patricia Hill Collins.

Knowing Patricia Hill Collins

In one of my doctoral classes, I was assigned to read *Fighting Words: Black Women and the Search for Justice* (1998) by Patricia Hill Collins. I found the entire text compelling, but having been a long-time admirer of Sojourner Truth, I was particularly drawn to Chapter 7 in the book: "Searching for Sojourner Truth: Toward an Epistemology of Empowerment." Throughout her life, Truth moved within different class-based and racial groups to share her political messages. In this chapter, Collins refers to this moving within groups as travelling through "outsider-within locations":

> Because Truth lived in a Black woman's body, her position in the world certainly shaped her position on her world. A traveler, a migrant who transgressed borders of race, class, gender, literacy, geography, and religion largely impenetrable for African-American women of her time, Truth remained an outsider within multiple communities.... For her, resolving the tensions raised by her migratory status did not lie in staying in any one center of power and thereby accepting its rules and assumptions. Rather, Truth explicitly breached group boundaries. By selecting the name Sojourner, Truth proclaimed that specialization and movement were both required in legitimating truth claims. No truth was possible without a variety of perspectives on any given particularity. (p. 231)

I felt empowered by this passage because it helped to explain the complex reality in which Black women exist in America and, more specifically, within academia. I understood that by accepting my outsider-within locations, I have a racialized gendered viewpoint to which others are not privy and access to certain locations because of my gender, others because of my race, and still others because of the intersection of my gender and my race. The women in the DIVAS collective work together to help one another as we navigate these outsider-within locations. By meeting regularly, DIVAS' members provide professional and emotional support for one another. This support is crucial in helping one another "breach group boundaries" within academia and beyond.

The raw boldness of "Searching for Sojourner" prepared me to take on Collins's (2003) work, "Toward an Afrocentric Feminist Epistemology," which opened my eyes even further. She explained the difficulties that Black feminists face when writing and publishing within academia. I could relate:

> While Black women can produce knowledge claims that contest those advanced by the white male community, this community does not grant that Black women scholars have competing knowledge claims based in another knowledge validation process. As a consequence, any credentials controlled by white male academicians can be denied to Black women producing Black feminist thought on the grounds that it is not credible research. (p. 50)

I felt validated. Because I am Black and a woman, I have a particular way of "knowing" that is valuable and justifiable, and because of the intersection of my race and gender, I have a particular epistemological standpoint that colors how I interact with others and how I determine and see truth. My truth no longer needed validation; I was a DIVA Sista in the making. Meeting bell hooks helped me find a sense of focus and purpose; and coming into knowing Patricia Hill Collins emboldened me as an academic. I was ready to make my voice heard, ready to feel Joan Morgan.

Feeling Joan Morgan

I first heard about Joan Morgan at an American Educational Studies Association annual meeting I attended during my third year as a doctoral student. As soon as I returned home, I purchased and read her book, *When Chickenheads Come Home to Roost* (1999). Hip-hop feminism—WOW! Now, like I mentioned in my hip-hop vignette, I have always been a hip-hop feminist; however, I did not have the vocabulary to describe how I felt. I finally could verbalize why I *still* love hip-hop. I could also verbalize why I choose to not only continue to support hip-hop but why I also chose to conduct my dissertation research on its effects on my Black male counterparts[4] (see Tafari, 2013). I understood that through hip-hop, Black men have been crying out for a long time, and Joan Morgan (1999) concurs:

> As a black woman and feminist I listen to the music with a willingness to see past the machismo in order to be clear about what I'm *really* dealing with. What I hear frightens me… . When brothers can talk so cavalierly about killing each other and then reveal that they have no expectation to see their twenty-first birthday, that is straight-up depression *masquerading* as machismo. (pp. 72–73)

This passage in particular moved me. I agree and believe that it is about time we start paying attention to the real message in the music and start trying to understand the culture. As a Black woman, a wife, a daughter, an educator, and a DIVA Sista, it is my responsibility to "stand in the gap" and "work in collaboration, not competition" with my brothers as well as my sisters to ensure the perpetuity of our community and our people. I could "feel" from where Joan Morgan was coming. bell hooks gave me vision; Patricia Hill Collins made me strong; and Joan Morgan gave me assurance. I was not alone in my passion for hip-hop, and I was certainly not crazy for acknowledging its influence in my life as a powerful part of my journey—a journey that would soon lead me to the DIVAS.

Embracing the DIVAS

I met Dr. DIVA Toni during the second half of my third year as a doctoral student. She had recently defended her dissertation, and we had been matched to carpool to the Southeastern Association of Educational Studies conference. As we talked on the long drive, she told me about DIVAS. I was intrigued as she explained how they support one another, socialize, and network. Furthermore, I was impressed as I learned more about DIVAS and how they had based their mission on Guiffrida' s (2005) othermothering framework. "Othermothering" was another one of those terms for which I did not have a name, but I had experienced. Yet here I was, again, at a transformative point in my life, in need of someone to show me some light (without even knowing it), and here enter the DIVAS, helping to dispel my "feelings of impotence through illustrating historical nontraditional patterns of empowerment for Black women" (James, 1993, p. 52). I was eager for the support, eager for the sisterhood, ready to feel empowered, and becoming a DIVA was incredibly empowering. They did not *tell* me that I could do it (be successful in the PhD program); they *showed* me. They stood present as living, walking counter-narratives who answered my questions, prayed for me, and laughed with me.

The DIVAS collective demonstrated, through a neatly woven framework that is composed of eight essential components, exactly how empowerment looks. There is some overlap among the components, but three aspects of this framework speak most loudly to me.

Organizational Structure That Empowers Members

The DIVAS Collective has an organizational structure that is caring, just, and inclusive, and can best be described as "servant-leaders" (Greenleaf, 1982). DIVAS members serve first and focus primarily on the growth and well-being of people and the communities to which they belong... . The servant leader shares power, puts the needs of others first and helps people develop and perform as highly as possible. (Greenleaf, 1982)

Every individual member who wants to serve can. I joined DIVAS two years after its founding; they had an executive board and several officers in place; however, I immediately felt included. I could relate to their passion for service. It was not long before my own passion for community organizing was recognized, and (when I was ready) I was appointed as the DIVAS community outreach coordinator. In this position, I manage our social-networking efforts: I share advice and helpful tips for members of the community who are navigating the doctoral process. I also share "DIVAS News" and updates about the members of the collective who have successfully passed their comprehensive exams, defended their dissertations, presented at conferences, etc. Finally, I also spearhead our efforts to reach out and offer mentoring and guidance to undergraduate women of color who are interested in pursuing graduate study (my absolutely favorite part of my "job"). Hence, in my position as community outreach coordinator, I am "paying it forward": empowering those around me as I have been empowered by those who came before me.

Voluntary and Fluid

Because participation in DIVAS is voluntary and fluid, I was able to take the time to figure out how to fit the DIVAS into my already hectic life. It was important that I not take on anything that was going to place any additional pressure on me—or take my focus away from completing my doctoral studies. I could only take on a project that was not only aligned with my professional goals but also had flexible participation requirements. The DIVAS were wonderfully understanding as they knew firsthand the rigors of doctoral study. They followed my lead, encouraged me to "check in" at least once a month to ensure that I was on target, and they were exceptionally loving and supportive whenever I surfaced from my writing dungeon.

System of Accountability and Responsibility

Though the DIVAS collective operates within a framework that is voluntary and fluid, there is also a strong system of accountability and responsibility. I found it encouraging that even though in the beginning I could not regularly attend meetings or events, I was still paired with a "Big DIVA Sista" who served as my mentor and advocate. She checked on me to offer her support and advice. When I began to experience overwhelm and doubt, she "stood in the gap" (Guiffrida, 2005) and lifted me up with emotional support, reassurance, and tough love (Reay, 2000). She helped me to develop a writing schedule and held me accountable for sticking to it. She proofread papers for me and shared constructive criticism. My Big DIVA Sista helped me prepare for my exams. And when she took a faculty position in another state, another one of my Big DIVA Sistas stepped up to ensure that I was prepared for my dissertation defense. Through this tightly woven system of accountability and responsibility, the DIVAS refused to let me fail.

As Black women, we share "an alternative epistemology" (Collins, 2003, p. 53) that reflects the landscape of our experiences inside and outside of the academic realm. This is what bonds us. This is what keeps us strong. This is what makes us servant leaders who extend our arms to offer a structured yet voluntary web of support for one another. Thus, I am grateful that when the DIVAS embraced me, I was smart enough to embrace them back.

Being a DIVA

Words cannot truly express what the DIVAS have done for me. However, from being a DIVA, I have learned the importance of paying it forward. Therefore, I find it necessary to share some parting words of love to those of you interested in or already pursuing a terminal degree. Four main concepts come to mind when I think about the actions that helped me to excel in my doctoral program:

- Seek out community
- Play the game by the rules
- Maintain balance
- Pursue your passion

Seek Out Community

My doctoral program was intense. There were not enough hours in the day to complete all of the assigned readings *and* write papers, but the community that I found helped my success (Murata, 2006). I engaged in conversation with the people in my classes with whom I shared common interests. We shared research ideas and presented together at conferences. We talked about outside interests as well, and we shared our dreams of "life after" the doctorate. I encourage you to build a community of people with whom to share your ideas, who will support and encourage you. Having this outlet will help keep you sane.

Play the Game by the Rules

I was an undergraduate when I first realized that success in college was, in large part, about politics and strategy (Jackson, 2004). In my doctoral program, I learned which professors meshed well with my learning style and personality. I paid attention to their teaching styles and did not attempt more than two exceptionally rigorous classes in the same semester. I learned about the professors' research interests and carefully crafted my dissertation committee. These are the people who will lead you through your comprehensive exams and dissertation process, so make sure you get along with all of them. Even further, make sure they get along *with one another*. Finally, listen to them. Once you have selected them, trust them to guide you through your process, especially your dissertation chair. If you do not have a good relationship with your chair, or if s/he does not believe in your work, then change your chair. This is the game. Your committee's job is not to make obtaining the doctorate easy for you. Its job is to ensure that you have developed the level of expertise and persistence to succeed in academia. Once you've been hooded, write your own rules!

Maintain Balance

Before I applied for my doctoral program, I sat down with my husband and asked him if I had his support. When he answered affirmatively, I clarified *exactly* what "support" meant: it meant that he would have to cook dinner more often and take our daughters to their extra-curricular activities. When he confirmed that he would support me, I moved forward with my application. When I started my doctoral program, I promised myself that I would stay married. This was not easy, but I was successful in keeping that personal promise. I have been asked on many occasions, "How do you maintain balance? How did you do it with a husband, small children, and a full-time job?" Sometimes I laugh and say, "I don't know!" However, I do know. First, I had to decide that I was committed to maintaining my family structure throughout the program. Then, I had to be proactive in that maintenance (Prakash, 2012). For example, instead of reading in my home office, I would read in the room with my daughters while they watched television. I would drive them to their three-hour Girl Scouts meetings, find a quiet room in the church, and work. Now I admit that being in the room with my children or at the church during Girl Scouts could sometimes be distracting; however, I refused to miss out on five years of their lives while I pursued this degree. My family needs my attention—all of them—and they deserve it, so I tried my best to be present in their lives while in my doctoral program. I also suggest maintaining balance with your social life. Though I had to scale back my level of participation, I still attended sorority meetings. I chatted with my girlfriends on my way to and from work. By keeping in touch with my family and friends, I was able to maintain the relationships that I had built before the doctorate and still achieve my academic goals.

Pursue Your Passion

All of the networking, politics, and balancing school and family will not be worth it if you are not pursuing something about which you are passionate (hooks, 1994). I was one semester into my program when I had my epiphany. I realized that I was passionate about the crisis affecting Black boys in schools, so I started trying to figure out possible ways to help them. I thought about the fact that there are so few Black men present in elementary school to help aid in their development, and I felt a strong compulsion to learn more about this group of teachers: Black men who teach elementary school. Then, I decided to tie in my passion for hip-hop (see Tafari, 2013). Because I was truly interested in this topic, and I believed in the importance of my work, I was motivated to keep going. Even when the going got tough, even when I fell into that "dark place" and did not want to write any more, I felt an embodied, visceral need to complete my process. If you can discover your passion early in your program, then you can begin to build your literature base long before you reach the dissertation stage. Thus, you can truly become the expert on that topic.

Conclusion

The journey from the Boogie Down Bronx to the Doctor of Philosophy has not been an easy one. However, it is a road well-travelled due to the love, support, and encouragement of my village. In this chapter, I have acknowledged different parts of myself by telling stories in the form of vignettes. The five vignettes illustrate how I came to love hip-hop, meet bell hooks, know Patricia Hill Collins, feel Joan Morgan, and embrace the DIVAS. Then, I shared what being a DIVA Sista meant to me and offered four tips that might help someone in any stage of the doctoral journey. I am proud of my journey, proud of my success, and most proud to be a DIVA!

Notes

1. Hip-hop was "born" in 1973 in the Bronx, New York, when DJ Kool Herc began to loop dance breaks at his sister's birthday party (Cook, 1985; Dimitriadis, 1996). From this moment, a movement was born. Black and Puerto Rican youth fervently embraced and utilized this movement as a platform that incorporated robust and artistic visual, physical, and verbal forms of expression. Hip-hop very quickly became the "CNN of the ghetto" (as Chuck D of Public Enemy once referred to it) as Black and Latino youth verbalized their frustrations with failing public schools, forced ghettoization, and a deleterious welfare system (George, 1992). Since its inception, hip-hop has grown beyond New York City project walls and has morphed into an international culture.

2. Joan Morgan coined the term "hip-hop feminist" in her poignant text *When Chickenheads Come Home to Roost: A Hip-Hop Feminist Breaks It Down* (1999). According to Morgan, hip-hop feminism is a "feminism that [allows] us to continue loving ourselves *and* the brothers who hurt us without letting race loyalty buy us early tombstones" (p. 36). Hip-hop feminists are "the daughters of feminist privilege" who "can't imagine our lives without access to birth control, legalized abortion, the right to vote, or many of the same educational and job opportunities available to men" (p. 59). Most importantly, hip-hop feminism is a voice that is committed to "keeping it real": a voice "that samples and layers many voices, injects its sensibilities into the old and flips it into something new, provocative and powerful" (p. 62). Since 1999, there have been several notable works published on hip-hop feminism by women like Gwendolyn D. Pough, Aisha Durham, and Andreana Clay, to name a few.

3. In the mid-1990s, the style of dress for video girls morphed. While dancers of earlier hip-hop wore biker shorts and baggy jeans in videos, the newer style required that they now wear bathing suits and micro shorts at an increasing rate. The norm had become that more of the female body would be exposed in videos.

4. Most of the Black men who I know and love (my husband, my brother, my cousins, my friends, my students) have experienced intense relationships with hip-hop. For me, hip-hop is one pathway to better understand many of the urban Black men around whom I was raised and/or have come to know in one way or another. Moreover, through hip-hop, I can oftentimes hear a Black man's pain, his frustration, his love, his passion, his fury, his desire.

7. Transition—"Changing the Game": The Role of Qualitative Narratives in Research and Knowledge Construction

CHERREL MILLER DYCE AND TONI MILTON WILLIAMS

It is important to note that qualitative inquiry is not formulaic but multifaceted and includes life history, autoethnography, and portraiture among many other forms. Interwoven like fabric on a quilt, these DIVA narratives present an epistemology that is grounded at the crossroads of research and practice. Essentially, the stories are their constructed realities, seasoned with passion, authenticity, and validity. These are true counter-narratives that underscore the question "Who decides which stories are valid?" and as such creates a new paradigm in social science research where "narrative and story as we imagine them functioning in educational inquiry generate a somewhat new agenda of theory-practice relations" (Connelly & Clandinin, 1999).

In capturing and generating new knowledge, these stories are our attempt to engage in open dialogue with a broad audience that might not as a practice read research-laden text. It is our vision that our words touch the very soul of the readers, not just their intellectual being. Thus, by employing various qualitative methodologies, we pay homage to Sarah Lawrence-Lightfoot's (2005) sentiments that:

> The newly emerging eclecticism is also related to changes in the audience for the researchers' work. Many of us are wanting to expand our audiences and welcome more voices into the public dialogues about education and schooling. If we want to broaden the audience for our work, then we must begin to speak in a language that is understandable, not exclusive and esoteric...a language that encourages identification, provokes debate, and invites reflection and action. But

> it is not only the language and idiom of our texts that will change, it is also that in anticipating different consumers of our work, we will begin to conceive of our research (the questions and design) differently from the very beginning. (p. 9)

Our stories are great examples of Black women taking scholarly authority by centering their stories and experiences qualitatively, thereby rejecting the positivistic paradigms that value objectivity, numerical supremacy, and rigidity. Instead, these narratives echo the unique standpoint of Black women educators who fully understand that our reality and epistemology are often best understood through our lived experiences and narratives, not devoid of emotions, voice, Afrocentricity, and culture. Collins (1999) unpacks the role of methodological selection in research and knowledge claims, and questions the criteria used in positivistic paradigms, its prominence in the academic research, and whether it truly provides agency for Black women and our experiences. She posits:

> Such criteria ask African-American women to objectify themselves, devalue their emotional life, displace their motivations for furthering knowledge about Black women, and confront, in an adversarial relationship, those who have more social, economic, and professional power than they. It seems unlikely, therefore, that Black women would use a positivist epistemological stance in rearticulating a Black women's standpoint. Black women are more likely to choose an alternative epistemology for assessing knowledge claims, one using standards that are consistent with Black women's criteria for substantiated knowledge and with Black women's criteria for methodological adequacy. (p. 755)

Each of the DIVAS uses her personal story as a means of hope, freedom, and liberation from positivistic ways of knowing. Denzin and Lincoln (2005) remind us that "qualitative researchers study things in their natural setting, attempting to make sense of, or interpret, phenomena in terms of the meaning people bring to them" (p. 3). These DIVA narratives provide a perspective of the doctoral experience that is relevant to the sociocultural, economic, political, and spiritual context that were integral in navigating the doctoral process. The narratives remind us that there is not one truth, and that "objective reality can never be captured" (Denzin & Lincoln, 2005, p. 5). Yet in our truth, we recognize that we can use theory to tell our stories while remaining true to ourselves.

8. *The Liberatory Educator: Transforming Lives, One Student at a Time*

Temeka L. Carter

As Charlie stood before my Bikram yoga class for the first time perfectly fit, radiant, and confident, I thought about how her very presence was liberating to me. She looked like a real-live Disney fairy, straight from Pixie Hollow, but most unlike the Tinker Bell character type. Even though her yoga wear resembled a Tinker Bell costume, it was slightly altered with spaghetti straps and cheetah print. This robust woman was unique in that she embodied a new-age fairy prototype: a tastefully tattooed, dark-haired bohemian with the temperament of the approachable and wise monarch Queen Clarion. From my vantage point, Charlie's character would make a wonderful addition to the fairy franchise.

In addition to her illuminating aura, what she said at the end of class as we were cooling down in shavasana greatly impacted me. The last relaxing pose of the 90-minute session usually ended with nature sounds emitting from a stereo while students finished meditation and headed to the dressing room in staggering fashion. On this particular day, however, Charlie lowered the volume and spoke into our lives as if she were a garden fairy sprinkling pixie dust on flowers to ensure their growth and vitality. As I lay on a mat resting and focusing on a breathing technique, Charlie's strong, clear voice echoed throughout the room to recite a familiar poem. She said:

> Our deepest fear is not that we are inadequate. Our deepest fear is that we are powerful beyond measure. It is our light, not our darkness that most often frightens us. We ask ourselves, Who am I to be brilliant, gorgeous, talented, fabulous? Actually, who are you *not* to be? You are a child of God. Your playing small does

not serve the world. There is nothing enlightened about shrinking so that other people won't feel insecure around you. We are all meant to shine, as children do. We were born to make manifest the glory of God that is within us. It's not just in some of us; it's in everyone. And as we let our own light shine, we unconsciously give other people permission to do the same. As we are liberated from our own fear, our presence automatically liberates others. (Williamson, 1992, pp. 190–191)

As she spoke, I absorbed every word, drifted deeper into meditation, and became keenly aware of the present moment as it was unfolding. It felt like I was having an out-of-body experience while listening to an old poem with new ears, but with profound resonance this time. The meditation stirred memories of personal challenges and fears that I had to overcome in my educational plight, and I suddenly felt grateful and strong. As I slowly regained consciousness, stood up, rolled up my mat, and walked to the dressing room, I knew with certainty that my struggles were not in vain. In fact, conquering them helped to inform the visionary, liberatory professor that I have become. I believe that my very presence in the classroom, like Charlie's in the Bikram yoga class, is liberating for some students, for my purpose and passion as an educator is to help light the path and show the way.

I did not plan to become an educator. If anything, intellectual curiosity serendipitously guided me along this career path. As a rising high school senior, I had very few plans except to exit my southern, rural, racially segregated community. I wanted this place where I'd felt estranged for most of my life to be far behind me in a rearview mirror, as a distant memory of a former life, or a blur in my consciousness. It was during elementary school, in the first grade, that I initially experienced educational alienation and the sting of what I call "the normalization process." A highly energetic, precocious child was not necessarily welcomed by most of the overworked, underpaid teachers who did their best to maintain order and accomplish the basic learning goals and objectives in the classroom. Needless to say, I was tremendously bored. Although I had excellent grades, my consistently low conduct scores caused teachers to deem me as disruptive—even a troublemaker. I would finish assignments quickly and then have to sit and patiently wait for classmates to finish. Instead of teachers providing me with more challenging assignments and cultivating my excitement for learning, I was misunderstood, misdiagnosed, and penalized. I experienced pain each time teachers asked a question and my raised, waving hand was purposely overlooked. The punitive treatment caused me to slowly become disenchanted and disengaged with school. It was not until I was given an opportunity later in that school year to live with an aunt in Detroit that I observed the vast differences in my educational experiences.

Not only did my enthusiasm for learning return at this new school, it increased tenfold, especially because I scored high enough on a placement exam to skip the second grade altogether.

Living in this racially diverse metropolitan area for a brief stint of my elementary school years was pivotal to my cognitive development and juxtaposition of life in the North and South. When I moved back to Alabama two years later, a grade level ahead of former classmates, I was able to better connect with nurturing teachers, but social dynamics in my hometown were relatively the same. Few White teachers and even fewer White students were present at my school. Essentially, Blacks and Whites lived, worshipped, and learned in two separate worlds. Limited social opportunities in the area made it easy for me to immerse myself in a newfound passion and means of escapism—reading.

Solving mysteries and proving hypotheses was an exciting, adventurous life that I lived vicariously through Nancy Drew, the Hardy Boys, Sherlock Holmes, *Matlock*, *Murder, She Wrote*, and other such books and TV shows. Although none of the highly perceptive protagonists looked like me, I delved into their fictional worlds and honed critical thinking and problem-solving skills. Reveling in the work of these investigators allowed me to accept my own questioning, curious nature as a strength and even a gift. Although off-putting for some of the people I interacted with, I simply loved thinking critically, asking questions, and discovering truths. One of my major interests centered on trying to understand the roots of racial segregation and Black socio-economic suppression. I wanted to know if this pattern was endemic to the South and areas of marginal development or if it was simply the way of the world. I explored the works of Black authors such as Maya Angelou, Toni Morrison, Richard Wright, Lorraine Hansberry, Zora Neale Hurston, and Langston Hughes in search of identity, meaning, and progress. I deeply desired to uncover material that absolved Blacks from perpetual obscurity in the world. For me, this was a great mystery to solve, and I was on the case.

Just around the time when I began exhibiting self-confidence in my social interactions and accepting the deeply religious training that I had received all my life, a family incident in the fifth grade rendered me voiceless and despondent. Blindsided and pushed to the periphery of my wits, I mentally detached from anyone relatively close to me, although I felt compelled to maintain a strong outward appearance. In such a small community, the last thing I wished was for my family to be shrouded in controversy and public ridicule. The hodgepodge of sincere indifference that I demonstrated towards everyone generally resulted in me feeling sheer awkwardness much of the time. Overall, I preferred to be left alone, for I was no longer my former self, and

I have never been since. In efforts to overcome my problems, I was advised to just talk to God. In my bitterly cynical mind, this suggestion only sounded like an ethnic sequel from Judy Bloom, *Are You There God? It's Me, Temeka*. During this crucial time of deep existential angst, I remarkably discovered the practice of journal writing, which allowed me the freedom to explore feelings and channel grief. As my only means of therapy, journal writing became a central part of my existence, an unmitigated safe space where only I was in control.

In efforts to endure my tenure in this complicated environment, I prided myself on managing a busy schedule, as I did not want my idle mind to become the devil's workshop. I remained an avid reader and journal writer throughout middle and high school. I participated in many church events, clubs, and organizations, all of which provided excellent leadership training and social development opportunities. In what previously seemed like millions of light-years ahead, graduation from high school was fast approaching, and I didn't have any concrete plans for the direction of my life. For years, I had exhausted energies to maintain a façade, to redirect, mask, and suppress my emotional issues without giving adequate attention to who I was at the core and what I wanted out of life. My fragmented self was in desperate need of repair, and the best I could offer it was an exodus. I accepted the first full college scholarship presented to me, in a random discipline. When I graduated on a Friday evening, my bags were fully packed and I eagerly anticipated leaving my hometown to attend summer school the following Monday morning. College was only four hours away, but the distance would provide enough space for me to rediscover myself and begin the healing process.

However arduous and revelatory, the life lessons I gained over a five-year period of undergraduate studies at an HBCU (historically Black college or university) are priceless experiences that have allowed me to better understand myself and my relationship to the world. During this time of discovering individual and group identity, it was crucial for me to interact with a mostly Black national and international demographic. The soccer team at my university attracted people from around the world, and I had a rare opportunity to interact with many international Black students and *see* myself, my varied Blackness, represented on the world stage through their shared stories and experiences throughout the Diaspora. The rich cultural context that my school provided (socially and academically) helped to reignite some of my childhood passions about exploring Blackness, and these experiences made all the difference in my decision to pursue graduate studies over attending law school.

Graduate school at a different HBCU was the most gratifying educational experience in my life because I was totally focused and finally had an opportunity to study the literature of African Americans in depth. My professors and classmates, most of whom were Black, engaged in powerful, challenging discussions as we juxtaposed past and present struggles and accomplishments, while simultaneously envisioning an equitable society for all people. Understanding the lives and challenges of remarkable individuals whose shoulders I stand upon, who added to the collective consciousness that helped grant civil rights and privileges I now enjoy, caused me to reevaluate my own plight in life. Because of my fervent desire to share and expand their wisdom, strength, and guidance with others, I realized that becoming an educator was a natural fit for me. This pragmatic career choice would make it possible for me to continue researching and studying, while also helping others to understand social dynamics. However, to effect change in the most significant way, I knew that I had to reach beyond my comfort level and knowledge of the Black community to engage with a larger, multicultural society. In retrospect, the time I spent in my mostly Black quasi-nationalistic environments strengthened my growth and development. In a discussion on connecting Black struggles for group survival, Bernice Johnson Reagon, founding member of the female musical group Sweet Honey in the Rock and longtime social activist stated, "At a certain stage nationalism is crucial to a people if you are going to ever impact as a group in your own interest. Nationalism at another point becomes reactionary because it is totally inadequate for surviving in the world with many peoples" (Reagon, 1983, p. 358). In efforts for me to evolve as an educator, it was time for me to go to the next level of my academic journey. Renowned scholar, feminist, and social activist bell hooks encourages teachers to participate in higher levels of social engagement in her book, *Teaching to Transgress: Education as the Practice of Freedom.* She says, "To teach in varied communities not only our paradigms must shift but also the way we think, write, speak. The engaged voice must never be fixed and absolute but always changing, always evolving in dialogue with a world beyond itself" (hooks, 1994, p. 11). I excitedly embraced the change as I carefully considered my next career move.

After graduating summa cum laude and teaching for approximately three semesters, I applied to only one PhD program that I felt served as an umbrella for all of my interests. Rhetoric and Composition seemed broad and marketable enough to secure a teaching position, but most important, I could remain engaged in the field of study because it aligned with my love for communication in all facets and for all purposes. I believed that proficiency in Rhetoric and Composition could yield unlimited possibilities for me to cultivate personal and social change through the classroom, for this is the work I mostly aspired to do.

Early in my doctoral program, I once again experienced educational alienation attributed to "the normalization process." Unlike in elementary school, I wasn't being disregarded because of overachievement; this time, I was being looked at *because* of it. Normalization within higher education took on a different meaning. It now meant that I had to produce expected doctoral-level work, regardless of having exclusively attended public, historically Black educational institutions all my life. I had to earn the academic respect of my professors (I was relatively comfortable with them, although none were Black like me), my peers (many of whom had traveled around the world and graduated from top-notch colleges and universities), and my students (many of whom had never been taught by a Black person, ever). Furthermore, with this school being my first PWI (Predominately White Institution) experience, I had to acclimate quickly for survival and success. Undergoing this rapid social growth process allowed me to truly experience W. E. B. Du Bois's (1903/1989) notion of double consciousness,[1] whereby I was constantly aware of the manifold implications of my Blackness and how others perceived me, both real and imagined, in relation to how I saw myself. It was an ongoing battle to rid myself of my eerie doppelganger who appeared during the most conspicuous times to shake my confidence and steal my voice. The apparent warring of my spirit revealed fears and insecurities that had to be addressed, sooner rather than later. I felt that talking with the other few Blacks in my program about my internal struggles would have been counterproductive, as they grew up in either diverse or majority White environments. It would also have been potentially costly, as academic programs sometime breed competitive students who employ underhanded antics to advance or get noticed. Belonging to DIVAS, a supportive group of non-competitive Black graduate students who understood my concerns at the PWI, could have allowed for better guidance and a smoother transition for me. However, the DIVAS collective did not yet exist. Consequently, I learned to navigate within this diverse academic environment through trial and error, which has positioned me to extend advice to future students with concerns about acculturation and graduate work.

Overall, my doctoral student experiences forced me to face prevailing fears and evolve into a self-proclaimed liberatory educator, which is discussed at length in Paulo Freire's *Pedagogy of the Oppressed* (originally published in 1970). He defines emancipatory or liberatory education: "This pedagogy [pedagogy of the oppressed] makes oppression and its causes objects of reflection by the oppressed, and from that reflection will come their necessary engagement in the struggle for their liberation" (Freire, 2000, p. 48). Furthermore, he affirms my belief of rigorous inquiry in the classroom by stating:

> Education either functions as an instrument which is used to facilitate integration of the younger generation into the logic of the present system and bring about conformity or it becomes the practice of freedom, the means by which men and women deal critically and creatively with reality and discover how to participate in the transformation of their world. (p. 16)

As a teacher who once felt penalized for being intellectually curious in primary school, I now embrace the challenge and opportunity for meaningful inquiry in my classroom. I passionately want to help liberate students' minds and transform them into wholesome, personally responsible, and productive citizens. In efforts to make this happen, I have to be constantly prepared to fully explore the possibilities of a more idealized educational experience, one that focuses on the individual and collective needs of the students, appeals to their multiple intelligences and sensibilities through current technologies and experiential learning, while simultaneously engendering a sense of community and civic responsibility.

Christian Weisser (2002), in his book *Moving Beyond Academic Discourse: Composition Studies and the Public Sphere*, encourages teachers to view their role in the classroom as having a trickle-down effect. He reminds us that we come in contact with many students who might move into positions of social power and authority. If we train them as critical thinkers and enable them to *read* their own lives, develop their own opinions, and respond in thoughtful ways, then we will have affected many individuals over the course of our careers, for "our work in the classroom might be seen as perhaps the most important and effective avenue of political and social change that is available to us" (Weisser, 2002, p. 127).

It is my belief that most students desire to learn, regardless of the subject matter. However, the way in which information is presented can determine the success or failure of engaging with students. It is my objective to use education as an urgent and necessary tool to stimulate, motivate, and encourage individuals to think critically and creatively. In the classroom, I strive to provide a forum where every voice is heard and valued, where students and I become partners in inquiry, learning, and evolving together.

Teaching is part of my life's journey of understanding human conditions to effect positive social change, and it is also a means of personal discovery and recovery efforts. Therefore, the classroom is never a comfortable site for me. It is always a test site in which I aspire to become more effective in methodology. It is a space of resistance, vulnerability, and growth. Literacy expert Mary Louise Pratt (1991) calls the classroom the "contact zone," for it is "intended in part to contrast with ideas of community that underlie much of the thinking about language, communication, and culture that gets done in the academy" (p. 37). Therefore, many traditional or socialized ideas are challenged and many students initially resist new ways of thinking. While teaching, I don't proclaim to have all the answers, not even most of them. Students and I learn and evolve together. I consider myself more of a facilitator of learning by providing students with the right atmosphere and tools to achieve success.

Like Paul Loeb's (2004) book title, I too believe *The Impossible Will Take a Little While*. I am encouraged by students' thoughtful and engaging interactions. I am hopeful that as I work to build one community at a time in the classroom, students will model the same principle and inspire others within their small communities. I agree with Loeb (2004) that "hope isn't an abstract theory about where human aspirations end and the impossible begins; it's a never-ending experiment, continually expanding the boundaries of the possible" (p. 223). All of my personal and educational experiences leading up to earning a PhD have liberated me to know myself more intimately and to use information as a means of creating and connecting the dots for living a more intentional, purposeful life. As a liberatory educator, it is my aim to inspire and transform students to impact their worlds in positive, meaningful ways.

A few years after graduation, I learned about DIVAS and gladly joined the Distinguished, Intellectual, Virtuous, Academic Sistas. It was rewarding to finally connect with a supportive, non-competitive group of Black doctoral students and post-graduates that I had longed for while in school. I could now seek and give advice without fear or judgment, for the DIVAS hold each other up and cultivate a spirit of excellence for our communities and ourselves. The beauty of belonging to this group of dynamic women is that each of us is strong in our own right and yet we *choose* to form a space away from the gaze of others[2] and combine our energies for a larger labor of love, inside and out of the ivory towers. For me, belonging to this group is a form of social activism and resistance; it is a positive counter-narrative of Black women in the United States. Patricia Hill Collins (2000) poignantly speaks about the importance of Black women's activism in her book *Black Feminist Thought*. She states:

> The challenges for U.S. Black women across diverse social classes consist of revitalizing institutions of Black civil society so that they can counter situations....
> If African-Americans ourselves cannot identify with Blackness, then why would anyone else value it? If U.S. Black women cannot put ourselves in the center of

our own intellectual and political work and claim identities as Black women, then who else will? (p. 223)

I personally appreciate how the DIVAS promote an African ethos of oneness, interconnectedness, and uplift, which are exemplified within the book titles *I Am Because We Are: Readings in Black Philosophy* (Hord & Lee, 1995) and *Still Lifting, Still Climbing: African American Women's Contemporary Activism* (Springer, 1999).

With Black women PhDs representing less than 4% of educators in the United States,[3] I view the work of DIVAS as an esteemed opportunity to ground Black women in a love ethic, which bell hooks (2001) describes in the introduction to *Salvation: Black People and Love:* "To give ourselves love, to love blackness, is to restore the true meaning of freedom, hope, and possibility in all our lives" (p. xxiv). The unparalleled wisdom, leadership, and opportunities offered through this female PhD cohort help to illuminate the lives of its members and the lives of people we interact with, for we are stars—shining, twinkling, and guiding together. As our light shines, we unconsciously give other people permission to let their lights shine also.

Advice for Black females considering a PhD program
(from Ruiz's (1997) *The Four Agreements: A Practical Guide
to Personal Freedom*):

1. Be impeccable with your word.
2. Don't take anything personally.
3. Don't make assumptions.
4. Always do your best.

Notes

1. In *The Souls of Black Folk*, W. E. B. Du Bois (1903/1989) describes double-consciousness: "It is a peculiar sensation, this double-consciousness, this sense of always looking at one's self through the eyes of others, of measuring one's soul by the tape of a world that looks on in amused contempt and pity. One ever feels his two-ness—an American, a Negro; two souls, two thoughts, two unreconciled strivings; two warring ideals in one dark body, whose dogged strength alone keeps it from being torn asunder" (p. xxvii).
2. W. E. B. Du Bois's (1903) use of *gaze* suggests, among all things, that the African American's attempt to gain self-consciousness in a racist society will always be impaired because any reflected image coming from the gaze of white America is necessarily a distorted one, and quite probably a harmful one as well.
3. National Center for Educational Statistics (2010)

9. An African American Woman's Continued Fight for a Pedagogical Education Inside of the Classroom

MARRISSA R. DICK

Education is a defining moment when epistemology and terminology equate to an epiphany, thereby igniting praxis.

— Marrissa R. Dick

Introduction

My primary school years were spent in Catholic school, and these educational foundational years were the most oppressive and abusive (mentally, emotionally, and physically) educational years of my life. Daily my emotional, physical, and psychological well-being was placed in the hands of nuns who believed that educational banking and oppressive authoritative measures were the necessary prerequisites for learning. This institution was located in the heart of Bronx, New York's African and Hispanic American community and it was operated by White nuns. These nuns never once demonstrated a loving attitude toward me, nor did they provide a safe environment. Instead they displayed aggressive behavior toward me, assaulted me physically on a routine basis, and verbally abused me.

As a child I always wondered why I was seemingly singled out to be physically and verbally abused by my teachers while I was in school. I understood early on that my family name (Dick) was at the root of it. My father's name is Mr. Charles Wayne Dick and my mother's name is Mrs. Joyce McClure Dick, so is there a big wonder that my name would have been Miss Dick? I remember clearly a nun glaring at me, a 7-year old child, with hateful, squinted blue eyes and with a venomous tongue tell me, "I hate having to say your name! It disgusts me!"

Faith is an essential component to my journey, and a passage of sacred text reminds us that "unto the pure all things are pure— but unto them that are defiled and unbelieving is nothing pure; but even their mind and conscience is defiled." I remember thinking at that moment, "You're a nun and my teacher. You're supposed to protect me." Marcus Tullius Cicero, the Roman philosopher, once stated, "The authority of those who teach is often an obstacle to those who want to learn" (2013, para. 15). I believe that my experiences in Catholic school were an intentional malicious obstacle meant to thwart my very being for success at life. In Trotman's (2009) article, "The Imposter Phenomenon among African American Women in U.S. Institutions of Higher Education," she reminds us of Johnetta Cole's keynote address at Smith College. Cole (1997) admonishes:

> In our country ... all black folks are doomed to be intellectually inferior to all white folks. Thus, the last image that many Americans would have of an African American woman is that of an intellectual, an academic, a college president, a person of the academy. (p. 77)

In my opinion my primary educators were doing their best to keep this hegemonic practice enacted through education.

It wasn't until I entered my doctoral program that I felt embraced by education. Through my first doctoral course, I understood that pedagogy is at the very core of learning. I now understand that pedagogy encompasses the heart of the teacher, the entire learning experience of self-actualization, the design of the classroom, and the inclusion of the curriculum, along with the mental and physical safety and well-being of the student. As an autoethnographer and qualitative researcher I can pose myself as the researcher and subject, which puts me in a unique position to explain my life story as I perceive it. Patton (1985) explains that

> Qualitative research is an effort to understand situations in their uniqueness as part of a particular context and the interactions there... . What it means for the participants to be in that setting, what their lives are like, what's going on for them, what their meanings are, what the world looks like in that particular setting. (As cited in Merriam, 2002, p. 5)

In addition, Smith (1997) supports qualitative research as exceptional when he says that qualitative research is a "special case of life writing" (p. 288) because it permits a life story to be conveyed in the context of theory and praxis from the individual's perspective.

My individual perspective as a doctoral student provided me with the terminology to understand my experiences with education and linked me to a sisterhood that extrapolated upon my ontological educational experiences. In this chapter, I introduce my initial experiences with education in the form of racial-microaggression experiences, I explain my introduction to racial micro-aggression inside of the classroom and how I understood its relevancy in my educational tenure, and I explain my relationship with the DIVA collective as an illuminating intercessor and othermothering voice during the final phases of my doctoral degree.

DIVAS Enlightenment of Racial Microaggression

In the first chapter of this book, "Standing in the Gap as the Academic Inter-cessor," Cherrel Miller Dyce asks two questions: first, will there be anyone to lend a boot, intercede, and model success in an academy where Black women represent a small percentage of the population?; and second, will there be anyone to perform what Guiffrida (2005) calls othermothering, a concept denoting the role of mentoring, support, and connection in the academic persistence of African American students? My response to these questions is a resounding yes, and it is called DIVAS.

One of the DIVAS' essential components is embodying a system of ac-countability and responsibility that empowers its members, in that when in-formation is gained from one of the members attending a conference, that DIVA has the responsibility of sharing that information with the group. It was this sharing of information that gave my life yet another revelatory answer to my mis-educative experiences and heightened my appreciation for being a part of such a body of scholarly Black women. At this particular meeting the vice president of the DIVAS, Dr. Toni Williams, had attended a conference where racial microaggression had been discussed. When she shared her expe-rience at this conference, I immediately understood its meaning and was able to position its definition in my life. As she shared the definition of microag-gression, my mind reflected back upon the many intentionally oppressive ex-periences that I had endured inside of the classroom at the hands of my teach-ers. Toni passed me her brochure and as I read it I knew without a shadow of a doubt that I had indeed been exposed to its forces. Here again my doctoral experience and my membership in the DIVAS collective was bringing validity and clarity to my oppressive educational experiences.

When the meeting concluded I went home anxious to research this new terminology. I discovered that an American psychiatrist, Chester Pierce (1974), first coined the term microaggression in 1970. He explains microag-gression:

> These [racial] assaults to black dignity and black hope are incessant and cu-mulative. Any single one may be gross. In fact, the major vehicle for racism in this country is offenses done to blacks by whites in this sort of gratuitous

> never-ending way. These offenses are microaggressions. Almost all black-white racial interactions are characterized by white put-downs, done in automatic, pre-conscious, or unconscious fashion. These minidisasters accumulate. It is the sum total of multiple microaggressions by whites to blacks that has pervasive effect to the stability and peace of this world. (p. 515)

Since then other ethnic scholars such as Derald Wing Sue (2010), an Asian American psychologist and guru of multicultural counseling, have conducted vast research on intentional and unconscious racism by Whites in society. In his book *Racial Microaggressions in Everyday Life: Race, Gender and Sexual Orientation*, Sue (2010) recognizes Chester Pierce's (1974) research on unconscious racism by Whites in American society. Pierce believes that "specific interactions between those of different races, cultures, or genders can be interpreted as small acts of mostly non-physical aggression"; furthermore, he states that microaggression is "the chief vehicle for racist behaviors" (p. 515). After concluding my research, I knew for certain that I had indeed been exposed to nuns who either intentionally or unintentionally exhibited racial-microaggressive behaviors towards me on a routine basis while I was in a learning environment. I now understand that it was the intersectionality between race, gender/sexuality, and religion that provoked the daily microaggression from the nuns. Had I not been a part of this group, I feel almost certain that I would not have been exposed to this terminology as I have not been exposed to the term since; however, I see the definition clearly and practiced daily within our society. I thank the DIVAS for holding true to their essential component of responsibility.

Juxtaposing Othermothering and Otherfathering—the DIVA Way

It is evident that my primary teachers practiced a racial-microaggressive educational attitude toward me instead of imparting and/or utilizing "othermothering" skills to provide me with a holistic and pedagogical educational experience. Collins (2000) teaches us that othermothering is "unlike the traditional mentoring so widely reported in the educational literature, this relationship goes far beyond that of providing students with either technical skills or a network of academic and professional contacts" (p. 191). Due to the fact that I withstood intentional educative oppressions, continued to better myself through education, and became a member of a collective body of Distinguished, Intellectual, Virtuous, Academic Sistas who have postured themselves as intercessors and othermothers in my life, I now possess the appropriate language and have the cognition to better understand my educational and life experiences.

In being enveloped by othermothering through the DIVAS, I now possess the wherewithal to juxtapose my experience with "otherfathering." Without being a part of this rich collective, I am not sure I would have ever equated the two terms. As Miller Dyce described in Chapter 1 of this book, an academic intercessor is concerned with moving Black students from the margin to the center (hooks, 1986) as they progress through their doctoral studies. My maternal grandfather was such an academic intercessor. Lee Ivory McClure lived in my parents' home while I grew up. Gramps, as he was affectionately called, was a self-educated man and was my first academic intercessor. Rarely did I ever see him not reading two books simultaneously—the Bible and the Encyclopedia Britannica. It was his "otherfathering" that fostered my relationship with education. He taught me at a very early age about Africa, Egypt in particular, because that society was richly advanced in technology and science. In his role as otherfather, Gramps taught me about slavery, the middle passage, religion, racism, and double-consciousness so that when I entered school I was well advanced beyond my peers in history (Black history in particular) and religion. If we were to take a look at otherfathering from a spiritual standpoint, we would most likely find that many religious advocators view otherfathering as the primary role in a child's life. While the biological father brings the son into this world, it is the religious mentor who brings the son into the next world. "A Torah teacher is like a father. A Torah teacher is greater than a parent!" (Student, 2012, para. 3). Religious educator Dr. Gerald Blidstein sees the otherfathering role within the community as an even greater role than the biological parent:

> ... this is not a pragmatic comparison, that the Torah teacher [teaches] to the spiritual which is greater than the physical world. Rather, the Torah teacher is also a father. And in choosing between fathers, you should choose the father who brings you into the greater world. (as cited in Student, 2012, para. 4)

It is the aforementioned standpoint that my grandfather adopted toward me. When I returned home from school, Gramps would be sitting at the kitchen table drinking coffee and eating dry toast. He would have a notebook and a pencil ready to write down my response to his daily question, "What did you learn today?" I would tell him what I learned in each one of my classes and watch him take notes. Once he finished we would do my homework together and then he would begin to dispel the untruths, in particular, about history and religion. He would ask me thought-provoking questions such as who occupied the Americas prior to Columbus coming to its shores. I would answer, "The Native Americans." The he would say, "Since they were here first and had cultivated the land, how could America be discovered when people were already living here?" After we had a discussion he would cross through that note and continue on to the next untruth. It was Gramps's desire that I learn to question what I was being taught. What he did not know was that my asking those questions in school was considered rebellious and disrespectful, and was cause for physical punishment. So instead of voicing what I learned from Gramps, I accepted and adopted an educational banking method while at school and appreciated the holistic, pedagogically sound, and emancipatory education I received at home. Michael Stone (2000) the author of *Talking with Dinosaurs*, who has performed extensive research in emancipatory education and critical thinking, writes that critical thinking is

> The kind of thinking which challenges fatalism, prejudice, apathy and indoctrination. The aim is to engage active citizens in informed participation in social and political life to achieve a more equitable and socially just democracy. Critical thinking is not simply concerned with overcoming individual and group 'ignorance' but with encouraging ways of thinking that are critical of the kind of status quo which supports inequalities, injustices and the abuse of power. (p. 26)

In receiving an emancipatory education from my grandfather and experiencing libratory learning during my doctoral program, I have been able to develop a capacity for critical reflection that I believe is essential for the development of higher-order thinking. Also, the DIVAS collective has afforded me the wherewithal to intellectually grapple with the inequalities in academia while at the same time providing me with encouraging ways to successfully navigate through its parapets.

What my grandfather did for my mind resembles Collins's (2000) "mothering the mind" theory. She explains that othermothering involves relationships that can develop between Black othermothers and other females who effectively become their students. This is exactly what I was to my grandfather—his student. It is in this vein that he felt compelled to tell me that history is written by those who concur. That statement was pivotal and poignant to me because it was in that moment when I understood even as a child why the history books rarely had anything positive to say about people who looked like me. In *Black Spirituality and Black Consciousness* (1999), Carlyle Fielding Stewart III shares that

> Having made these significant contributions historically has generated only a modicum of interest for white historians and intellectuals, for to laud the achievements of blacks is to refute the myths of black inferiority and black incompetence

and to shake the foundations of white America's racially hegemonic and debilitating mythologies. (p. 52)

During that same conversation, Gramps also told me that within my womb I possessed the cradle of civilization and at the same time informed me that that same womb held the matrix for slavery. He introduced me to the multiple and competing ways that White America pigeonholes African Americans and how they maintained a hegemonic stronghold past slavery to secure their social dominance and monetary capital within society. What my grandfather was doing is comparable to Swigonski (1996) contrasting the Afrocentric worldview that "attempts to dispel misconceptions and distortions about people of African descent. Furthermore unlike Eurocentrism, Afrocentrism purportedly offers an optimistic and holistic frame of reference that is not ethnocentric because it does not 'claim or aspire to hegemony'" (p. 55).

In his seasoned years of experiencing life as a Black man in America, he was well versed in racial inequality; therefore, Gramps was adamant that I would embrace my smooth honey-brown complexion and braided hair, and not despise it. Likewise I can embrace my DIVA Sistas because every woman in the collective has lived life as an African American woman and has experienced the same social injustices as I have. In this collective there is no need for clarification. The social injustices and inequities in academia and life are merely understood. It was important to my grandfather that I not possess a double-consciousness and view myself or my heritage through a skewed lens. In *The Souls of Black Folk*, W. E. B. Du Bois (1903/1989) talks about the concept of double-consciousness in that African Americans are only capable of seeing themselves through the eyes of White America. Du Bois (1989) is earnest when he postulates

> a world which yields him no true self-consciousness, but only lets him see himself through the revelation of the other world. It is a peculiar sensation this double-consciousness, this sense of always looking at one's self through the eyes of others, of measuring one's soul by the tape of a world that looks on in amused contempt and pity. One ever feels his two-ness—an American, a Negro; two souls, two thoughts, two unreconciled strivings; two warring ideals in one dark body, whose dogged strength alone keeps it from being torn asunder. (p. 23)

Due to the fact that I am now an educated woman, I can extend Du Bois's premise and hypothesize that Black women possess a triple consciousness because we are Black, we are American, and we are women. I am thankful to the DIVAS collective for introducing me to Guiffrida's (2005) concept of othermothering as it relates to expanding relationships, assisting biological parents with sharing the mothering responsibilities, social uplift and socialization, and inviting an interconnectedness of student learning. In my opinion, through otherfathering, my grandfather, Lee Ivory McClure, epitomized these concepts and it is the relationship that I have with my DIVAS sisters that brought to light this association of othermothering and otherfathering.

Emancipatory Educational Practices

It pains me to wonder if I had never entered a doctoral program or been asked to join the DIVAS collective if I would have ever found my "better and truer self." Du Bois (1903/1989) articulates that the Negro can "merge [her] double self into a better and truer self" (p. 3). In recognizing my truer self through education, I can immediately recognize when there is a difference in my educational space and when my teacher's posture toward teacher-student interaction is one that is genuine and welcomed.

In my graduate program I was exposed to the philosophies of John Dewey and other progressive and humanistic educators; however, it was Dewey's educational philosophy that initially liberated and provided me with the academic terminology to understand my former educational experiences. In his book *How We Think*, John Dewey (2010) shares with educators that it is the teacher's responsibility to harvest the students' learning, not to thwart it. He says:

> A gardener, a worker of metals, must observe and pay attention to the properties of his material. If he permits these properties in their original form to dictate his treatment, he will not get anywhere. If they decide his end, he will fixate raw materials in their primitive state. Development will be arrested, not promoted. He must bring to his consideration of his material an idea, an ideal, of possibilities not realized, which must be in line with the constitution of his plant or ore; it must not do violence to them; it must be their possibilities. (pp. 197–198)

Just as clearly as I can recall the multiple accounts of physical abuse I endured in elementary school, I can equally recall my first holistic and pedagogically sound course as a doctoral student. In this instance education was a meal for my body, mind, heart, and soul. It was a delicacy where the dessert was served first. My doctoral program was the genesis of my holistic relationship with education. In my constant and reflective state, in particular, when it comes to education I am very aware of my surroundings as well as those who profess to be teachers. Once I realized that my professors welcomed and appreciated my questions, I entered my doctoral classes enthusiastic and ready for engaging dialogue. In the past I had routinely been chastised in front of my classroom peers for asking "too many questions." I also endured harsh and abusive comments from my teachers, such as, "What is wrong with

you?!"; "Are you really that stupid?!" and "Why do you ask so many questions?!" Hurtado (1996) argues that

> women of color must constantly be aware of what they say and how they speak
> within classroom settings because of the visible markers of race and gender. As
> such, scholars examining the academic experiences of women of color suggested
> that educational environments and classroom dynamics impact women of color
> differently than White women. (p. 5)

Needless to say, I was immensely embarrassed and these abusive statements
silenced my voice for a great portion of my educational years. In learning that
education should be transformational, my doctoral experiences have been just
that—life changing.

I soon began to recognize my doctoral experience as one of healing. I
remember the moment when the roots of all of my racial-microaggressive
experiences were uprooted. It was during a fall semester when I was taking a
course titled, ironically enough, "Introduction to Critical Pedagogy." At the
end of one of my classes, my professor touched me on the arm and asked,
"Marrissa, did I answer all of your questions? Are you clear about what I was
saying?" His concerned demeanor, the pleasant tone of his voice, the gentle-
ness of his touch, and the sincerity in his eyes began to erode all of the ugly
comments made to me by his scholarly predecessors. In that moment and
in that space, my professor had no idea of the years of pain he had begun to
heal. Steiner (1923) delivered a lecture at the Waldorf School concerning the
forces that lead to health and to illness in education. He shares:

> Often in classes, or the whole work of a school, one sees a certain heaviness, and
> this heaviness must be overcome. Such heaviness can also express itself in an arti-
> ficial enthusiasm. Yet this can never accomplish what is needed, but only that kind
> of enthusiasm which is kindled out of the way in which we ourselves enter into
> the material we are dealing with in the classes. And here it is necessary that we
> work toward the development of a special kind of consciousness.... . This we can
> do only if, deeply in our own hearts and not merely in external phrases, we come
> directly to a true experience of spiritual values in the field of pedagogy. (para. 2)

When I entered my home that evening, the memory of my interaction
with my professor was still very present with me. It felt like a warm blanket
wrapped around me as if I were sitting on my couch holding a cup of hot
chocolate with melting marshmallows on a quiet winter morning. Through
my tears, I was able to erase those teachers' faces, their names, their authoritative voices, their physical abuse, and their personal opinions. Due to that
pedagogical teacher-student moment, I am no longer haunted or intimidated
when I cross the threshold of a classroom; instead, I feel safe and most of all,

welcomed. Freire reminds us that "love is an act of courage, not of fear, love is a commitment to others. No matter where the oppressed are found, the act of love is commitment to their cause—the cause of liberation" (p. 89).

It is true that my prior experiences should have prohibited me from re-alizing my full humanity; however, the libratory praxis that my doctoral pro-fessor extended toward me provided a libratory space for me to re-create my lived experience so that I could create the space "which makes possible the pursuit of a fuller humanity" (Freire, 1970, p. 29). I believe I experienced a moment of transcendence through one teacher's pedagogical practice. As a Black girl, my first experience with education was neither holistic nor peda-gogically sound because it was served to me through the hands of microag-gressive nuns. Had it not been for my grandfather daily reinforcing my value as a beautiful and smart Black girl and providing for me a historic account of civilization and education through history books, encyclopedias, slave narra-tives, and maps, I have no doubt their attempts at thwarting my educational success would have triumphed. Years later as a Black woman I utilized educa-tion to heal my pain from old educational wounds and past life experiences. Now I possess the "Eros," the love of learning that bell hooks describes as transformational. hooks (1994) says:

> Understanding that Eros is a force that enhances our overall effort to be self-actualizing, that it can provide an epistemological grounding informing how we know what we know, enables both professors and students to use such energy in a classroom setting in ways that invigorate discussion and excite the critical imagination. (p. 195)

In Cynthia Dillard's (2006) book *On Spiritual Strivings: Transforming an African American Woman's Academic Life*, she reminds us that it is our responsibility to have self-definition. She writes:

> From an endarkened epistemological ground, all views expressed and actions taken related to educational inquiry arise from a personality and culturally de-fined set of beliefs that render the researcher responsible to the members and the well-being of the community from which their very definition arises. (p. 16)

In my opinion the DIVAS collective embodies her standpoint because this scholarly body of academicians has made themselves responsible for the well-being of other Black women in pursuit of the terminal degree.

The Academic Component of DIVAS

When I think about being a part of a collective, I think how fortunate I am to have been introduced to the DIVAS. It is not important that I was not there during its infancy state; what is important is that this professional group of Black women entered my life during a time when I needed the most help while on my academic journey. Prior to my comprehending and appreciating the value of othermothering, I was adopted by our vice president, Dr. Toni Williams, who volunteered to undergird me as I was preparing to defend my comprehensive exam. Another component of the DIVAS is a social and spiritual component. As such my DIVA sister Dr. Toni Williams and I would meet outside of the group at a coffee house to discuss the oral defense of my comprehensive exam. I found this such a selfless act, but then again this is what we as African Americans term "going beyond the call of duty" to make it happen for one so all can benefit. In fact, Fries-Britt and Turner Kelly (2002) noted that supportive Black faculty willing to go "beyond the call of duty" helped them succeed (p. 321). This is what Toni did for me as an othermother. She went beyond the call of duty to make sure that I would be successful in defending my oral comprehensive exam.

During these meetings Toni, our vice president, would ask me questions that pertained to my research and simply asked me to explain it. Not until these meetings did I realize that I was not nearly as adept in explaining my research as I thought I was. She simply explained to me that as a novice she should be able to understand what I was talking about, and she was right. At one of these meetings I was frustrated because the more I was able to explain my research, the more she would "poke holes" in my research. I began to wonder if I knew anything at all. Toni calmly told me that she was not intentionally trying to poke holes in my research, rather she would prefer for me to grapple with my answers in her presence than for me to stand before my dissertation committee unprepared to appropriately deliver an intellectual reply to their inquiries.

Guiffrida's (2005) research reminds us that

> Black faculty conveyed the message early on to them that Black students not only had to overcome burdens of being a minority at a PWI, but also that they must perform at higher levels than White students to be viewed equally. As a result, the Black faculty at this PWI indicated high expectations of their African American students and pushed them to succeed in their classes. (p. 712)

It was in this safe meeting space when Toni shared her personal testimony with me of how she did not pass her initial comprehensive defense. She looked me squarely in the eye and told me that she did not want me to have that experience. I remember inhaling deeply and thanking her for being honest with me. The truth of the matter was at that particular point I was not prepared to orally defend my comprehensive exam. In Green and King's (2001) article *Sisters Mentoring Sisters*, we are reminded of the fact that an academic sisterhood is "designed to provide Black females with the resources they need to develop a broad knowledge base, as well as specific skills and competencies, that will contribute to their success at all levels of the academy" (p. 2).

Toni and I had a couple more meetings and she finally told me she believed I was ready. That meant so much to me because truly in my heart I knew I finally was. So I went to my dissertation chair the following day and told her I was prepared. She asked me a few questions and without hesitation I was able to confidently and thoroughly articulate my thoughts. My chair instructed me to set up the defense date. Once I did, I informed my DIVA Sistas and immediately a prayer chain was lifted up. The day I defended is one I will never forget. I was asked a question by a committee member and in the midst of my answer I lost my train of thought. My heart began to pound rapidly. I closed my eyes, lowered my head, and called upon my faith to bring back a body of scholarly knowledge that I knew I had retained. I know without a doubt that the prayers of my family, friends, and DIVA Sistas aided in my remaining calm in that moment so I could regroup my thoughts. Faith and prayer are strong components of the DIVAS collective and I already knew that their prayers had preceded me inside of that room. When I raised my head and spoke I was able to clarify the question with such confidence and scholarly logos that the entire committee was astounded. I remember them looking at me with awestruck eyes. After that I was told that I had passed and each member signed my comprehensive form.

As I walked to the graduate school to submit my paperwork, I clearly remember thinking that if Toni had not "poked holes" in my research, I would not have been prepared to face my committee and all of this could have gone another way. In Chapter 1, Miller Dyce reminds us that

> A central component of the interceding process is to promote academic success of all Black women and to coach them towards completion, thereby upholding our DIVAS motto that "none will be lost." Within the DIVAS, othermothering allows us to search the hall of academe spiritually for our Black sisters, helping to lead them to the crossing.

I am one of those DIVAS who had a successful crossing because I had help from Toni and I had prayers from the collective.

In conclusion, I would hope that those who read this chapter have been able to identify any microaggressive educational or life experiences and understand from where it derives. It is my hope that any person who has experienced racial microaggression, and in education in particular, would somehow find the strength to continue seeking education and the rewards it provides towards a richer and fuller human life experience. In particular, for Black women reading this rich collective of works, know that you can glean some form of strength from our academic experiences and know that others have come before you who can help you. Know that you are not alone. I would encourage you to seek out a lifeline such as the DIVAS on your respective campuses or initiate one if such a collective is nonexistent because it was in belonging to such a strong collective of African American women that I have been undergirded through prayer, given advice on how to navigate my personal life with school, and taught the protocol of academia. One my best friends and DIVA Sistas, Dr. LaWanda M. Wallace, stated during one of our DIVAS meetings that "Hegemony is a hell of a drug" (L. Wallace, personal communication, May 23, 2014). Through the DIVA collective this "drug" is acknowledged and brought to the forefront so its ill effects in the academic arena can be banished from an already marginalized group of people.

The Distinguished, Intellectual, Virtuous, Academic Sistas have been a blessing during my doctoral pursuit. Thank you to all of my DIVA Sistas for being there for me. I cannot and will never, ever forget you. Peace and blessings.

10. Present, but Not Present: The Personal and Educational Journey of a Doctoral Student Experiencing Deployment and Divorce

LaWanda M. Wallace

Autoethnographer at Heart

My love for autoethnography prompted me to journal my experiences when working on my PhD while experiencing the detachment that deployment and divorce can bring. Journaling through the years and now looking back over them has given me the chance, as Grason (2005) says, to "jump off a few cliffs and reveal myself to another human being" (p. xii). In doing so, I have been able to reclaim my space in a world that is overly cluttered with confusion and secrecy. I choose to tell my own truth, as uncomfortable as it may make others. This is what is so amazing about autoethnography. It is never about the person reading it as much as it is the person telling it. I have found freedom in this.

I am an autoethnographer at heart. In simple terms, "auto" means from one's own perspective. Thus an autobiography is a piece of work that is written from and about the perspective of the person who is writing. "Ethno means people or culture; graphy means writing or describing. Ethnography then means writing about or describing people and culture, using firsthand observation and participation in a setting" (Ellis, 2004, p. 26). When "auto" is added to the word "ethnography," you then have autoethnography, which is to write about the culture of oneself in relationship to others. Ellis (2004) said it this way, "autoethnography refers to writing about the personal and its relationship to the culture" (p. 37). This type of writing has been around for many years, yet it gives new meaning to research done in a scholarly context.

Autoethnography is rooted in ethnographic research. "Stemming from the field of anthropology, autoethnography shares the storytelling feature with other genres of self-narrative but transcends mere narration of self to engage in cultural analysis and interpretation" (Chang, 2008, p. 43). Anthropologist Karl Heider is noted as the first to introduce this concept in 1975. His original meaning, however, had intentions of the term "self" to mean the informant rather than the researcher (Chang, 2008; Ellis, 2004); but through the years, "self" in autoethnography has grown to be associated with the actual researcher. This is noted in the history to be attributed to David Hayano who studied his own people (Ellis, 2004). Today, most autoethnographic researches follow Ellis's model, which places the focus on the researcher as the main participant.

Autoethnography invites authors to reach new plateaus and understanding of themselves. It pushes the writer to truly examine his or her experiences as they relate to others in the living world around them. Autoethnography is both complex and simple. It invites you to expose and expunge. Some could even argue that autoethnography can be therapeutic. It is for all of these reasons that I've found this chapter, and any other work that I've done like this, both challenging and rewarding.

Introduction

Sisterhood has its privileges. I cannot remember exactly when, but I didn't find DIVAS, it found me. I was introduced to the group during the early stages of its conception and whereas I can't say I attended the very first meeting, I have been a beneficiary of the hard work and the vision that was set forth on that day. For that I am thankful. I began my journey with the Distinguished, Intellectual, Virtuous, Academic Sistas at a time in my life when having a group of likeminded women to connect with was a joyful want, not a necessity. Little did I know how much that would change.

In 2010, I began the early stages of a divorce, and the support group that I once thought of as a joyful want became a desperate need. A divorce, much like a dissertation, will change you forever. Having a group that can help with this change is invaluable. This chapter, in part, discusses my educational journey as a doctoral student who experienced deployment, divorce, and finally a completed dissertation. Special emphasis will be placed on the DIVAS and how the social and spiritual component and the system of accountability changed my outlook on my process and forever bonded me to the collective.

Stateside Deployment—Bound by War and Others

Although I have never held a gun, put on combat gear, or trained for war, I have served at the pleasure of my country stateside. Unfortunately, military life confronts families with demands that exceed the life of normal families (Karney, Loughran, & Pollard, 2012). One of the most common demands is paying the price for freedom. Because freedom is not free, it certainly put a strain on not only my marriage but my educational journey. Besides the constant and unwavering fear that I felt for my loved one, I was left with maintaining my household and working through the strain due to deployment-induced separation (Mansfield et al., 2010). This emotional strain caused me to rarely if ever make it to any DIVA meetings. I attended class physically but mentally I was never there. My concern was not as much on deconstructing societal norms as it was reconstructing a sense of normalcy in my life.

The deployment process itself is inherently stressful for military families (Lowe, Adams, Brown, & Hinkle, 2012), and this stress is undoubtedly intensified when a spouse has been left behind. There is a void that is left that is unmatched to most. Ironically, both the soldier at war and the family member at home pay the price for freedom. In paying this price, a sense of mental imprisonment is created. It is in this space that I found myself during the early days of the deployment and the dissertation. I was, and in some ways remain, bound by the expectations of others; bound by the pressures of the academy, and most important, bound by accepting the role of a divorced individual and what that means to my identity. All aspects of my life are paralleled to this and my position within the academy as a junior faculty. In some ways I am still trying to be set free.

Present, but Not Present

The idea of being physically present but not mentally present is a precarious one. Faber, Willerton, Clymer, MacDermid, and Weiss (2008) label this concept as ambiguous presence that occurs when a family member is perceived as being physically present but psychologically absent. Because I was in school, I was around people on a daily basis. I was physically present, but emotionally I was always detached and drained. "The psychosocial burden on families of deployed military personnel is less well understood" (Mansfield et al., 2010, p. 102), and even more so by people who have never experienced it. I never felt a part of my current environment. I never truly felt like I belonged. People around me were worried about finishing their next paper or chapter and I was worried about getting a phone call in the middle of the night from or about my loved one. People tried to console me and empathize with me, but I knew nobody truly understood, which at times made their concern feel empty. Spouses are more likely than service members to report that stressors of life or emotional problems have impacted their work (Hoge, Castro, & Eaton, 2006). My school work was affected and suffered greatly because of it. People wanted me to be a part of their world but my understanding of life beyond the borders of our country would not allow me.

Life became even more strained once my partner returned home from war. This was mainly due to the fact that the military does not require an extensive debriefing for soldiers and families postwar. As human beings we change and grow day by day. The intensity of this change after being apart for over a year was magnified and greatly attributed to my divorce. The readjustment period coupled with divorce made the thought of my dissertation being completed seemingly impossible. With all of these stressors, it should never come as a surprise that military families have one of the highest divorce rates.

Jumping from One D to the Next

I have spoken a great deal about how deployment affected me educationally and also what divorce did to that experience. What I have not discussed, however, is how I truly made it to the dissertation stage. Moreover, how I successfully completed it. For more than a year I grappled with the idea of completing my comprehensive examination—partially because of time, but mainly because of the fear that I had of being alone with my thoughts. Completing the comprehensive examination is a major step that must be done before you can get to your dissertation phase. Doing so in the state of mind I was in made it even more challenging.

When one sits down to write, one has to be in the most creative space possible. A writer must be in their clearest mind because in that space she is expected to generate new ideas and formulate stronger ways of understanding the world in which we exist. Every researcher must take ownership of her own work and must be sure to be inclusive of evidence that supports or denies her claim.

> Every speaker-as-writer has an obligation to develop a personal style that brings meaning and morality into discourse. This will be done through intonation, inflection, pacing and word choice. This style is political and conflictual. It refers to how something is morally expressed. A text should show, not tell. (Denzin, 1997, p. 40)

In transitioning from my comprehensive examination stage to the dissertation stage, I found developing this writing style most difficult. It was during this time that I made my way back to DIVAS through the regularly scheduled meetings, but not in a traditional sense. My Big Diva Sister would meet with me individually. Initially the meetings started off about work but soon adjusted to more personal aspects of our lives. Essentially, we created a sub-community outside of the larger one that already existed, in that we were able to form a bond, which ultimately laid the foundation for me to trust my personal experiences with the DIVAS. It was during this time that I began to redevelop my voice and reclaim my space within the circle.

Because I Had *To*

I found myself at the crossroads where I questioned whether I *wanted* to finish my process or whether I felt I *had* to, and decided that the latter was accurate for me. It was something about going to the next level in my educational journey that I inherently felt was tied to my overall destiny of my life. There were many days that I did not want to pick up a pen, let alone open up a book to do work, but I *had* to.

My professors were patient with me at first but just like any *othermother*, they too had their limits on the slack I had allowed myself. The same is true for the DIVAS whom I connected with and even my friends who were not a part of the academy. After many years of making excuses, I began to lose patience with myself. Although I was legally divorced, mentally I was not as detached. It was not until I decided that I no longer wanted to continue my mental hiatus that change occurred.

On September 22, 2011, I stepped out on faith. I decided to quit my full-time job, take a graduate assistantship, and finish school. Some days I questioned if it was faith or simply being foolish. I always settled that it was definitely faith. I sent the following message to my sisters:

> When I entered graduate school, it was always the plan that when I got to the writing stage of my program that I would step away from my program. This plan seemed clear and easy when we were together. Now years later and by myself leaving my job and pursuing my education while serving as a graduate student is a little scary, BUT I know that's what I'm being called to do. He has proven to me time and time again that He is in control. I don't know what else to do but to trust in or believe but that.

I had run long enough, and it was time to finish what I started. Now that I was focused, I knew that nothing could stop me, not even my past. I was not clear on how I would finish, but I knew that my life depended on it.

Successfully Overcoming

I know that not every story has a happy ending, but this one does. Seven months after leaving my full-time position, I successfully passed my oral defense for my comprehensive examination. Something that I had prolonged for more than two years was over and done just that quickly. Less than a year later, I was sitting before my committee successfully defending my dissertation, and two months after that I was walking across the stage, which has yielded to me the best day of my life so far. There is hope.

When I initially submitted the title of my chapter many years ago, I was doing so to be vindictive. I intended to write it in a very different way. This is an ugly truth that I don't want to admit. Now years later, I have written my chapter and told my story because I have embraced it. I'm not ashamed of it. I don't choose to hide it. Most of all, *I* think of myself differently because of it. I am clearer about who I am not only as a woman but as a person of color in the academy. From my perspective, this is what DIVAS is all about: making space for women of color in a place where space does not always exist and being unapologetic for being perceived as different even though we understand that different is actually the norm. Finally, being free to express who we are according to *our* standards. We understand each other. Collins (2000) states, "Although racial segregation is now organized differently than in prior eras, being Black and female in the United States continues to expose African-American women to certain common experiences" (p. 23). Black women themselves can only truly understand these experiences.

My process was extremely difficult, but it helped to shape me; thus, I would not change one thing about it. I believe that it is not about how you start, but how you finish. I finished strong. My experience as a doctoral student taught me valuable life-changing lessons such as perseverance, strength, forgiveness, and patience with others and myself. My doctoral process taught me that I was not perfect and that was okay. Coupling that experience with two deployments and a divorce, I know without a doubt that without a proper support group I would not be writing this chapter as Dr. but rather Ms.

Each of us came to DIVAS for different reasons, but we each need or needed it equally. For me it was and still remains the sisterhood. The other-sistering, or simply having sistas, has been the foundation that undergirds my process as I navigate the academy. It truly did take a village to get my PhD, and part of my village absolutely were the DIVAS. Having a group of women of color, more specifically Black women, has proven to be one of the experiences that helped me persist. The DIVAS as a critical community turned out to serve both my want and need for support. Caring together is the basis of our community. We don't come together simply to console each other or even to support each other (hooks, 2003). We come together because we need each other.

What Education Did for Me

Education did for me what scholars such as Plato (1992), Freire (2004), and Shapiro (2006) describe as the essence of education. It liberated me. Plato's work assumes that we are shackled at our neck inside of a cave staring at shadows on the wall cast by the light of a fire. We think that the shadows are reality, when there is a world of sunlight waiting for us outside of the cave (Plato, 1992). Essentially, how do we convince people to go outside? How do we inform them that life outside of the cave is good? That was my process and the DIVAS helped me to come away from the cave.

I will be forever grateful for my liberation and transformation. Revisiting this story only solidified that for me. If you are reading this and struggling with deployment, divorce, your dissertation process, or anything that is hindering you from completion, I beckon you to look into the sunlight. Stop staring into the flame. There is life on the other side.

Find a support group, like DIVAS, that can help you through. If there is not one that already exists, then create one. Some people make it through on their own, but most do not. Stay true to who you are, and understand that you may change. As you get further along in your process, you should. That is a good thing. Understand that you are not perfect, nor will your work ever be perfect. It is okay. The best advice I ever received from my mentor was *the best dissertation is a finished dissertation*. If you can accept this and understand that in finishing you're just beginning, then you have mastered the biggest part of the process. We are always undone. Those who know this know the secret to happiness and success. My deployment disconnected me. Although I did not see it at the time, my divorce disentangled me. My dissertation devoted me, but ultimately it was the process of everything that defined and changed me forever. Find your defining moment and change will come.

11. Through the Fire: Marked, but Not Burned—A Doctoral Journey Transformed by Life's Obstructions

KIM DOGGETT PEMBERTON

The above symbol is the West African Adinkra symbol Hye Won Hye,
which means "fireproof."
This symbol represents divine protection in times of need and crises as well as in good times.
In other words, in times of trouble, trials, and triumph, the divine forces will always
be there to protect the true followers.

Strength does not come from winning. Your struggles develop your strengths.
When you go through hardships and decide not to surrender, that is strength.
— Arnold Schwarzenegger

KINDLING: In the Beginning...

The idea of strength developed through one's struggle is easily and often stated, yet more challenging to attain. My DIVA story speaks of strength through the hardships I endured during the doctoral process that had little to do with my academic course, but more about the integral resilience that kept me from surrendering, even with the onerous luggage I was transporting along the journey. Growing up the only girl between two very athletic and sometimes rambunctious brothers helped to mold me early as an extremely tough and resilient "tomboy." I endured my share of black eyes, bumps, and bruises, along with a few trips to the emergency room as I tried to keep up with the guys. However, now I feel that those early challenges were my preliminary "boot-camp experiences" for what was divinely in store for me.

It was approximately four years after my initial diagnosis of pre-menopausal breast cancer that I decided to become a student again in a full-time doctoral program, while already serving as a full-time elementary teacher, mother, wife, and dance ministry director of my church. This decision placed additional accountabilities on my current extensive list of responsibilities, yet the support of family and friends stimulated me to follow this new dream. After all, the surgery, treatments, and aftereffects were behind me. That successful outcome empowered me to confront and conquer yet another challenge, and school was it.

This chapter, situated in Nash's (2004) scholarly personal narrative (SPN) framework, and the psychosocial factors (Erikson, 1956) related to breast cancer survivors and how this diagnosis may affect one's academic and social productivity, combines the accuracy and precision of traditional writing with personal experiences, placing me at the center of all that materialized around me during the journey—family, schoolwork, research, oncology appointments, and the DIVAS collective, which initially entered my life in the form of a non-DIVAS colleague and confidante (NDCC) named Cynthia. Furthermore, as this chapter reveals my experiences while pursuing a PhD, it also optimistically embraces the principles of the West African Adinkra symbol of imperishability and endurance, titled fireproof, or that which does not burn (pictured above). This symbol represents the overall protection of a Divine Force in times of need and crisis, as well as in good times. It gets its meaning from traditional priests who were able to walk on fire without burning their feet, which was an inspiration for others to endure and overcome difficulties (Document and Designs, 2012). Therefore, in times of trouble, trials and even triumph, the Divine Force will always be there to protect true followers. Though I am not a West African native, my own American heritage and Christian ancestry has taught me to embrace a divine being greater than myself to guide my path and strengthen me for the journey ahead.

Thus "Through the Fire: Marked, but Not Burned—A Doctoral Journey Transformed by Life's Obstructions" describes how my journey, in its divine orchestration, not only educated, empowered, and protected me for what I would endure, but it was in these struggles that I developed strength. This "in the storm" strength you will read about is intended to also endow others who have the desire to want more for themselves, even after the perils of life have infiltrated it. Thus, the resilience of the early "tomboy" years and the support of DIVAS, in a journey of their own, helped sustain me while I was in my own inferno.

DIVAS: My Psychosocial Combustion

Erik Erikson's (1974) psychosocial theory looks at how social influences contribute to one's personality throughout an entire lifespan. Psychosocial factors specify how we visualize and live out life's experiences (Erikson, Paul, Heider, & Gardner, 1959). This includes both psychological and social aspects of life, which positively and adversely affect an individual's capability to manage their day-to-day responsibilities (Erikson et al., 1959). According to Erikson (1974), humans are affected by life's experiences in two ways: through external and internal influences. The external influences are important parts of one's life that we have no control over. Internal psychosocial factors are also important. Yet internal influences are more difficult to observe and recognize because they are inside an individual and cause them to function properly, or not, in life's circumstances (Clark, Kotchen, & Moore, 2003).

After ten years of remission, positively experiencing cancer-free visits and examinations, I never imagined the possibility that the external factor of post-menopausal breast cancer (Colditz, Rosner, & Speizer, 1995) in my family would crossover into my pre-menopausal age bracket, and now, with so many roles to juggle, I could not fathom that this routine breast examination would yield me such devastating news AGAIN! I had experienced this a few years before entering the doctoral program, but hearing the mammography technician say, "Please come back for one more image" alerted me to the fact that this would be different—and it was. I was instructed to report in two weeks to a nearby surgical center to have the mass removed. Carrying on in the manner that my tomboy exterior prepared me for, along with the covering of the Hye Won Hye (fireproof-protection), I went about the next two weeks seemingly unaffected, but with much prayer.

My positive psychosocial factors included my immediate, as well as extended family, and later, upon its inception, also encompassed my DIVA Sistas. Although DIVAS was not created, I had DIVA support with Cynthia, my NDCC. We collaborated on many junctures—professional conferences, school committees, and even class performances. Through it all, we made a doggone good team! Thus it was our teamwork and Burnett's (2001) research on collaborative cohorts that sparked our verbal agreement/pact with one another, to go back to school and pursue a terminal degree together, so we could act as one another's support system during the doctoral process. Though Ryan, Stiller, and Lynch's (1994) research is related to the academic success of children in school when positive relationships are formed, it was this same cohort and relational success we anticipated merging us in our educational process.

Additionally, other psychosocial factors were my personal views and perceptions related to breast cancer and the new role that school would play in my life. Erickson (1987) also indicates that these factors are significant in dictating how a person thinks and behaves, and they define how well a person copes with the realities of crises and diseases such as, in my case, breast cancer. How would I handle my "new normal" as a survivor and student, included in my already long list of duties and responsibilities? Encouragingly enough for me was the fact that research verified how individuals who possess strong support networks are equipped to successfully navigate life's demands (Jairam & Kahl, 2012). As a result, I was properly equipped, because I had the support system to keep me encouraged and moving toward my new goal—a terminal degree (with little emphasis on the word terminal).

Engulfed: Graduate School and a Second Diagnosis

Upon returning to the classroom after almost two decades on the opposite side of the desk, as teachers and not students, there were times when the content felt like a disconnect for Cynthia and me. Based on our previous schooling, both of us with bachelor of science and master's degrees from historically Black colleges and universities (HBCU), the predominantly White institution (PWI) we attended challenged us differently (Erickson, 1987), though it definitely did not discourage our intellect. Therefore, at some point we both realized we were not making the same progress as the full-time doctoral students who had taken the pay cuts and given up their teaching positions. They received research opportunities as well as the full attention of faculty for questions and impromptu lunch sessions (Guiffrida, 2005). Was it our "invisible knapsack" (McIntosh, 1990) that separated us? The invisible knapsack is a term coined by McIntosh in her essay, "White Privilege: Unpacking the Knapsack," based on racial inequality. McIntosh emphasizes that these privileges are not distributed equally or shared by individuals of every race. As students, we were feeling totally left out of "the academic loop," but little did we know that another even more compatible support system for the doctoral journey of Black female students at a predominantly White institution,

DIVAS collective, was in its early stage of conception and would soon avail itself to us, providing the scholarly support that was furthermore necessary for routing this level of the journey. In hindsight, I can see how DIVAS was my Hye Won Hye (fireproof-provision), the divine forces that "charred" my new route.

Now, quitting my job as an elementary teacher was a topic I did not want to consider, even after the probing of my advisor and chair of my committee, but it became apparent that it was needed. Therefore, after a well-thought-out and written plan of leaving the elementary classroom for two years, my husband and I decided to take the financial plunge. I took an educational leave of absence, the term used by the school district where I worked, and that following August I became a full-time graduate assistant, working with pre-service teachers. We took out school loans to assist with the household bills (replacing my missing salary) as my graduate assistantship would pay my tuition. I worked diligently to stay on track with my academic schedule. It was during that semester (approximately five years into my doctoral process) that the cancer cinder burned its nasty self back into my breast and I had some significant decisions to make—mastectomy and recuperate at home for six additional weeks, or lumpectomy and quickly return to my studies. I chose the latter, with expectations to rapidly continue this journey, with my newly found three R's—research, rewriting, and radiation. Thus, I procured a new evacuation plan for finishing this process. It was my "in-the-storm" strength. In addition to my aforementioned R's, I personally had a vendetta on the R of retaliation, as the disturbing news of my initial diagnosis probably haunted my mother for months. This diagnosis was received on the anniversary of my father's defeat to the cancer demon (lung and pancreatic) several years prior. My battle was not a solo match; I was in it for all who loved me!

Conversely, after my second surgery, I considered myself still a contender in the battle, until my surgeon informed me of the need to return to the operating room (only two weeks later) to remove additional cancerous lymph nodes they later discovered. From there my research and writing went downhill as my summer served as recovery from the surgeries, both physically and mentally. Thus my two-year doctoral plan had to be extended.

As I returned to responsibilities as a student and graduate assistant the next fall, I was told of a new group (later named DIVAS—Distinguished, Intellectual, Virtuous, Academic Sistas) being developed to support Black women on their PhD journeys. I knew once again that the Divine Force that kept me covered was clearing another path for me to continue this journey successfully. I attended the first meeting and was extremely impressed by the assurance by our current DIVAS leadership of support in the academy, knowing that was exactly what I needed to terminate the feeling of academic disconnect I was experiencing and to make me accountable to the work ahead of me (Guiffrida, 2005). Knowing that my NDCC, Cynthia, and I would reach even greater heights with additional sistas striving toward the same goal, we became original DIVAS (now comically referred to as ODs).

Research indicates that African Americans enrolled in PWIs often struggle with their relationship development as it pertains to the campuses' White faculty; therefore students of color often solicit academic assistance from family, friends, or teachers who are also individuals of color (Arnold, 1993; Fleming, 1984; Guiffrida, 2005). At this point, my doctoral journey changed for the better. As DIVAS, we met regularly to engage in academic discourse and understanding, to read each other's dissertation chapters, and prepare one another for written and oral defenses—we worked! Our DIVAS president, Dr. DIVA Cherrel, articulates that as liaisons for each other, our collective goal is to foster one another towards academic greatness with successful completion of the process and the mindset "to reach back and bring another sista into the doctoral fold." My first DIVA assignment was to present my research, which had been accepted at an upcoming National Reading Conference (now Literacy Research Association) to the group. The DIVAS collective required me to prepare my presentation and handouts, and to present my roundtable discussion before them in exchange for suggestions and constructive feedback. This is the epitome of what the DIVAS collective represents to each individual on this journey. After my mock presentation and the feedback I received, I was more than prepared for my first national conference presentation that consisted of my own research. Just as my academic efforts were supported by my family and Cynthia (who is now my DCC—DIVA colleague and confidante, because we are both founding members), my new DIVA family did also, which placed me in an even better position to reach my PhD goal. I now had supporters who were also on this journey. Moreover, my positive psychosocial factors, my tomboy manner of control, and my "fireproof" determination to be triumphant confirmed what Rose (1990) describes as the will/inner strength to win. They all evoked a fight in me like never before. I now felt ready to walk on the burning embers. The tomboy was determined to tough it out and be successful.

> Chemotherapy involves taking anti-cancer medicines by injection directly into a vein or by mouth in the form of a pill. Two or more chemotherapy medications are often given in combination. The medicines travel through the bloodstream to all parts of the body. It is given in cycles of treatment, followed by a recovery period. The entire chemotherapy treatment generally lasts several months to one year, depending on the type of drugs given. As chemotherapy damages the

cancer cells, it also can damage some of the body's healthy cells, which is why you may experience side effects (Cobb, 2013).

As treatments and medical appointments became a norm in this new life, the chemotherapy caused me to soon embark on the most horrific part of the ordeal for me—wearing a wig. Yes, you heard me—chemotherapy did not frighten me, needles did not deter me, and the pain seldom brought me to tears, but when a doctor mentioned hair loss, this superficially tough tomboy became a babbling basket case—to lose my hair was demoralizing. Yet I had Cynthia, my DCC, and another dear friend to go shopping with me to purchase my wig, which we named Lulu. I continued to be strong and in charge of my outlook on the disease while focusing on school. Not only did we shop for my new look, Cynthia and I took our research books and drafts of our writing into the cancer facility to occupy us during my chemotherapy treatments. Those three to four hours were not wasted on pain, tears, and sleep. We engaged in research dialogue, writing, and bouncing ideas back and forth. In addition to my research, I read to inform myself of the improved survival rates after a diagnosis (Ashing-Giwa et al., 2004; Chu et al., 1996) as motivation and inspiration. Therefore, I progressed with the plan to stay as much in control as I could. I declared that this once-proclaimed tomboy would not concede to *fighting like a girl*. Both my medical and academic experiences kept me grounded in my faith.

As I progressed with my schoolwork and dealt with the cancer, honestly there were times when I wanted to share my diagnosis with faculty so I could slow down and rest my body, but the tomboy refused that route. My goal was to "suck it up" and continue the journey, even if it meant masking my physical and emotional exhaustion. Later, I distinctly remember the strong and direct counsel of our president, Dr. DIVA Cherrel, at a meeting, warning us that "personal issues have no place in academia." As those words rang in my ear, I smiled inwardly, pleased that my actions met the approval and the matter-of-fact advice shared by our president. I did however, out of obligation, feel the need to inform my chair of my medical circumstance. He seemed almost as distraught as I initially was, as we had developed a relationship with my research discussions. My confidentiality was kept at school and I progressed in the manner of privacy I desired.

Backdrafts: In the Home

A backdraft is an explosion caused by a fire, resulting from the rapid re-introduction of oxygen to the burning rubbish in an oxygen-depleted environment (Fleischmann, Pagni, & Williamson, 1993). In other words, just when you think the flames are out, here comes another gust of the danger. Well, such was the case for my journey. Many on the outside looking in thought my life had bounced back after the cancer with minimal changes from its original state, and physically I had mended remarkably; however, my home life had not mended quite as seamlessly. We were operating in our own silos, yet residing as a family in one dwelling. People tend to be more stressed at home than at work, because they try to juggle many responsibilities at once (Lee, 2014). That was definitely my role—the juggler! As such, the tension mounted, and my son and husband clashed on many occasions. This unhealthy explosion resulted in brutal punishments, and even a minor child with a strong sense of social justice/fairness brewing within him, being forcefully dismissed from the home to find himself rescued by extended family, until I could cease fire and douse the flames in an attempt to bring some peace back into the home.

On this particular backdraft occasion, the two males in my life exchanged words over chores, the unwashed dishes, and when my son refused to clean them because it was not his day; he was immediately dismissed from the home. As I drove up to the house late that evening, I saw him sitting on the front porch without a coat in the middle of January. As if that was not enough, this event was playing out on the very week my oral comprehensive exams were scheduled to occur. Would I need to reschedule them due to home issues? The earlier DIVA advice rang loudly in my head—*Keep your personal business out of the academic world. They don't need to know your problems.* The tension in the house was boiling as I went in as the white flag of surrender. It did not take me long to understand the resolve of my husband as he was adamant about "not letting him back in the house" this time. I knew I had to make a decision that was in the best interest of all of us. I knelt in the dark of my bedroom and cried out, "What must I do?" In seconds, my Hye Won Hye message was delivered. I had to find a place for my two children and me to stay. We relocated for the next three weeks until my unwavering request for family counseling was heard by my husband. During our displacement, no one other than my DCC knew of my circumstance. She drilled me over the phone with possible comprehensive questions and kept my mind focused on my academic process and not my immediate predicament. That morning, my twins and I prayed as usual, I dropped them off at school, drove to the university, and successfully defended my oral comprehensive examination, all while displaced from my home—again the Divine Force carried me through, because no one, not even Cynthia, knew our displacement location!

Additional Backdrafts: Yet Another Revelation

After a few family counseling sessions and heart-to-hearts with Cynthia, my twins and I returned to our home and family counseling turned into marriage counseling, as the problem resided between the two of us. Things again seemed better, but we all protected ourselves behind a firewall of caution. As counseling attempted to bring us closer, one infamous day I sat down at the home computer and discovered the messages that would perpetually pry us apart—an affair (certainly not the words he chose to describe his inappropriate relationship with another female). The emails, written by her, were startlingly exposed, right there on our home computer, which he obviously forgot to close out. The messages spoke of shared times, pet names, intimate feelings, and the fear of a dwindling relationship as she felt them drifting apart. The pit of my stomach probably touched my throat as I was truly scorched; yet, the tomboy in me would not cry. He lay asleep merely 20 paces away, down the hallway in our bedroom, yet I calmly replied to the emails, copying both of them and signing my message, "Wife of 17 Years." This was Hye Won Hye (fireproof-strength) at its highest level of control! No communication exposing the email transpired between us as he departed for work that evening, but I later received an "I messed up . . . we need to talk" text message. I assumed my email had been read. I had no words for him and the next few days were quiet, until another backdraft occurred.

With our mismatched work schedules, we only shared the master bed two nights weekly, as those were his off days. After the recent discovery, I was determined we would not sleep there together on the first night since the email revelation. As he retired for the night, I entered the room and requested his departure. We disagreed and what I thought to be a quiet, yet uncompromising face-to-face disagreement ensued; however, our teenaged son overheard our escalating voices and opened the bedroom door stating, "What are you doing to my Mom? That's a lady, man!" Again dousing the flames, I assured our son that I was fine. He reluctantly left the room and shortly after, so did his father. I kneeled to pray before retiring for the night and was disturbed by shouting. This time the backdraft was the result of an unhappy father who had just been emasculated by his teenaged son. The shouting turned into abuse and I made a 911 call. I eventually requested that my husband leave the home, because I felt his heart was no longer in the marriage or the fatherhood role he once held. He finally moved out. It was hard on the family, yet according to Wallerstein and Kelly (1981) the decrease of tension was, and still is, a bonus. Sure, we missed the family as it was, but that family had checked out long before this episode. However, during all of this, I continued to fulfill my teaching obligations as a graduate assistant. I not only had my two children to be concerned with, I also had a team of 27 pre-service teachers counting on me to see them through their student teaching and graduation. One does not do this alone. It takes a Divine Force to carry a load like this. It was actually at the DIVAS' holiday social, the day after my graduation, when I openly shared my marital situation (at that time, separation) with my DIVA Sistas. The compassion, prayer, and support that filled the room brought the tomboy to tears—tears of joy!

Smoldering: My True Revelation

No, the fires were not all extinguished, but the smoldering remnants revealed the divine plan for my children and me. We were all to gain some tomboy strength and join in on an intense faith journey with the Divine Force who keeps the promise to always be with us (Deuteronomy 31:6). My twins and I endured the hardships of the separation and the subsequent divorce through disconnected electricity, semi-bare cupboards, the threat of repossession of our only means of transportation, and even foreclosure on the home. My will was determined to keep moving closer to my goal. The DIVAS collective rallied around to support my efforts, not knowing my family situation. Their efforts were engrossed because they knew my clock with the university was ticking fast. My dissertation defense was in October 2010. I requested that all wear pink in honor of my breast-cancer fight while on this doctoral journey. What an awe-inspiring vision to see even my male supporters and committee chair dressed in pink. Additionally, the DIVAS collective supported me in a powerful custom on that day. Dr. DIVA Cherrel entered the room an hour before the defense to pray and enter in the powers of the Divine Force that was my protector and guide throughout the journey. The room began to fill with my support network. My defense is probably still known as one of the largest attended. My psychosocial network of more than 30 family members and friends, six of my DIVA sistas (Cherrel, Toni, Cheryl, Torry, Jolanda, and of course, Cynthia, my through-it-all DCC), and even my estranged husband all witnessed as I extinguished the last ember of my PhD process.

I am now on the smoldering side of this once-raging inferno, as the flames have been fully extinguished and the transparency of the smoke has unveiled much about my strength, my faith, my DIVA sistas, and the tomboy within me. Though my marriage did not last, my "in-the-storm" strength has been bonded to a higher being, my Divine Force, for life. Again, strength does not come from winning, because my marriage can be viewed, by some, as a loss. I often remark that in order to gain three additional letters at the end of my name (PhD), I relinquished the three letters I already had at the beginning of my name (Mrs.). Yet that was a divine destiny to "free" me and bring me into an intimate relationship where all of my needs are sufficiently met with favor, grace, mercy, and the fireproof support of my DIVA sistas.

Campfire Conversation: Advice to the Reader

Assuming that you have read this chapter because you are contemplating the road to a terminal degree, after some firestorms of your own, you may wonder where your doctoral journey will lead you. Here are my embedded lessons of advice.

Ground yourself. The road ahead can be long, winding, and rough. Ground yourself with a divine being higher than man, which can comfort and refocus you during the unexpected mishaps that attack your plan. This grounding ensures that you will stand a better chance of continuing toward your destination of successful completion. Solicit the prayers of others to strengthen your journey as well.

Establish a plan. This is your proposed blueprint that clearly details the life-transforming journey in which you are preparing to engage; however, you should also establish alternate routes in the event the original plan needs to be voluntarily or involuntarily altered. It is also important that this step is wisely and cautiously vetted with those special individuals (your psychosocial network) taking/sacrificing this journey with you.

Develop relationships. Do not make the mistake of thinking that this is a solo journey. Study groups, support systems, and individuals who know the doctoral road, need to be in your new networking database. These are not family and friends, but those who are on your committee as mentors and advisors as well as those who have crossed the burning embers on the same road, merely steps (semesters) in front of you. Their knowledge and experiences can better prepare you for what is yet to come.

Contain the personal. Though you must develop relationships on this journey, your personal dilemmas should not trespass on the doctoral relationships you have formed. You may not be able to fully separate your life issues from the academic aspect of this journey in your head and heart, but you must refrain from exposing the personal within the academic setting. In simpler terms—keep it to yourself.

Stay positive. This recommendation is self-explanatory. You must retain the positive mindset with which you began the journey. Though obstacles may set up roadblocks, barricades, and speed bumps, typically referred to as life, continue to believe in yourself, your journey, and your completion, because you CAN do it!

References

Albold, C., & Miller Dyce, C. (2011). A community of scholars: The role of a peer-based dissertation group in countering attrition and prolonged ABD status in doctoral students. *Perspective: A Newsmagazine for Graduate Admissions Professionals, 23*(4), 13–18.

Arnold, K. D. (1993). The fulfillment of promise: Minority valedictorians and salutatorians. *The Review of Higher Education, 16*(3), 257–283.

Ashing-Giwa, K. T., Padilla, G., Tejero, J., Kraemer, J., Wright, K., Coscarelli, A.,… Hills, D. (2004). Understanding the breast cancer experience of women: A qualitative study of African American, Asian American, Latina and Caucasian cancer survivors. *Psycho-Oncology, 13*, 408–428.

Aud, S., Hussar, W., Johnson, F., Kena, G., Roth, E., Manning, E., … Zhang, J. (2012). *The condition of education 2012* (NCES 2012-045). Washington, DC: U.S. Department of Education, National Center for Education Statistics. Retrieved from http://files.eric.ed.gov/fulltext/ED532315.pdf

Azor, H. (Producer). (1985). *The Showstoppa* [Recorded by Super Nature (Salt-N-Pepa)]. Philadelphia, PA: Pop Art Records.

Bair, C. R., & Haworth, J. G. (1999). *Doctoral student attrition and persistence: A meta-synthesis of research.* Paper presented at Association for Study of Higher Education Annual Meeting, San Antonio, TX.

Bandura, A. (1997). *Self-efficacy: The exercise of control.* New York: Freeman.

Bandura, A. (2001). Social cognitive theory: An agentic perspective. *Annual Review of Psychology, 52*, 1–26.

Barton, T. (2006). Feminist leadership: Building nurturing academic communities. *Advancing Women in Leadership Online Journals, 21*.

Beauboeuf-Lafontant, T. (2009). *Behind the mask of the strong Black woman: Voice and the embodiment of a costly performance.* Philadelphia, PA: Temple University Press.

Benson, J. E. (2006). Exploring the racial identities of Black immigrants in the United States. *Sociological Forum, 21*(2), 219–247.

Bernard, C., Bernard, W. T., Epko, C., Enang, J., Joseph, B., & Wane, N. (2000). "She who learns teaches": Othermothering in the academy. *Journal of the Motherhood Initiative for Research and Community Involvement, 2*(2), 66–84.

Besharov, D. J., & West, A. (2002). African American marriage patterns. In A. Thernstrom & S. Thernstrom (Eds.), *Beyond the color line: New perspectives on race and ethnicity in America* (pp. 95–113). Stanford, CA: Hoover Institution Press, Stanford University. Retrieved from http://media.hoover.org/sites/default/files/documents/0817998721_95.pdf

Bettez, S. C. (2011). Building critical communities amid the uncertainty of social justice pedagogy in the graduate classroom. *Review of Education, Pedagogy, and Cultural Studies, 33*(1), 76–106.

Biemans, H., Deel, O., & Simons, P. (2001). Differences between successful and less successful students while working with the CONTACT-2 strategy. *Learning and Instruction, 11*, 265–282.

Billson, J. M., & Terry, M. B. (1981). *In search of the silken purse: Factors in attrition among first generation students.* Presented to the Annual Meeting of the Association of American Colleges, Denver, CO.

Bourdieu, P. (1977). *Outline of a theory of practice.* Cambridge, UK: Cambridge University Press.

Bowen, D. M. (2012). Visibly invisible: The burden of race and gender for female students of color striving for an academic career in the sciences. In G. Guttierrez y Muhs, Y. Flores Niemann, C. G. Gonzalez, & A. P. Harris (Eds.), *Presumed incompetent: The intersections of race and class for women in academia* (pp. 116–132). Boulder: University Press of Colorado.

Brock, R. (2005). *Sista talk: The personal and the pedagogical.* New York: Peter Lang.

Bronfenbrenner, U. (1979). *The ecology of human development: Experiments by nature and design.* Cambridge, MA: Harvard University Press.

Bronstein, L. R., & Abramson, J. S. (2003). Understanding socialization of teachers and social workers: Groundwork for collaboration in the schools. *Families in Society, 84*(3), 323–330.

Brown, C. M., Davis, G. L., & McClendon, S. A. (1999). Mentoring graduate students of color: Myths, models, and modes, *Peabody Journal of Education, 74*(2), 105–118.

Brown, D. R., & Gary, L. E., (1991). Religious socialization and educational attainment among African Americans: An empirical assessment. *The Journal of Negro Education, 60*(3), 411–426.

Brown v. Board of Education of Topeka, 347 U.S. 483 (1954).

Bryant, V. (1999). The social construction of "manymothering": Representations among African-American Women. *Psychoanalysis and Psychotherapy, 16*(2), 235–260.

Bullock, H. A. (1967). *A history of Negro education in the South: From 1619 to the present.* Cambridge, MA: Harvard University Press.

Burnett, P. C. (2001). The supervision of doctoral dissertations using a collaborative cohort model. *Counselor Education and Supervision, 39*(1), 46–52.

Carlson, S. (2001). Distance education is harder on women than men, study finds. *The Chronicle of Higher Education, 48*(5), A48.

Carter, J. A. (2002). A dialogue with divas: Issues affecting a scholarly agenda in SPED. *The Journal of Negro Education, 7*(4), 297–312.

Cartledge, G., Gardner, R., & Tillman, L. (1995). African Americans in higher education special education: Issues in recruitment and retention. *Teacher Education and Special Education, 18*(3), 166–178.

Case, K. (1997). African American othermothering in the urban elementary school. *Urban Education, 29*(1), 25–39.

Chang, H. (2008). *Autoethnography as method.* Walnut Creek, CA: Left Coast Press.

Chatters, L. M., Taylor, R. J., & Jayakody, R. (1994). Fictive kinship relations in black extended families. *Journal of Comparative Family Studies, 25*(3), 297–312.

Cherlin, A. J., & Furstenberg, F. F., Jr. (1986). *The New American grandparent: A place in the family, a life apart.* New York: Basic Books.

Chiesi, H., Spilich, G., & Voss, J. F. (1979). Acquisition of domain-related information in relation to high and low domain knowledge. *Journal of Verbal Learning and Verbal Behavior, 18*, 257–273.

Chu, K. C., Tarone, R. E., Kessler, L. G., Ries, L. A. G., Hankey, B. F., Miller, B. A., & Edwards, B. K. (1996). Recent trends in U.S. breast cancer incidence, survival, and mortality rates. *Journal of National Cancer Institute, 88*(21), 1571–1579.

Cicero, M. T. (2013). *Cicero quotes.* Retrieved from www.goodreads.com/author/quotes/13755.Marcus_Tullius_Cicero

Clark, C. F., Kotchen, M. J., & Moore, M. R. (2003). Internal and external influences on pro environmental behavior: Participation in a green electricity program. *Journal of Environmental Psychology, 23*, 237–246.

Cobb, P. (2013, November 26). *Systemic treatments for ILC: Chemotherapy, hormonal therapy, targeted therapies.* Retrieved from www.breastcancer.org/symptoms/types/ilc/treatment/systemic

Colditz, G. A., Rosner, B. A., & Speizer, F. E. (1995). Risk factors for breast cancer according to family history of breast cancer. *Journal of National Cancer Institute, 88*(6), 365–371.

Cole, J. B. (1997). *Dream the boldest dreams: And other lessons of life.* Hong Kong: Longstreet Press.

Coleman, C. S. (1988). Social capital in the creation of human capital. *The American Journal of Sociology, 94*, S95–S120.

Collins, P. H. (1986). Learning from the outsider within: The sociological significance of black feminist thought. *Social Problems, 33*, 14–32.

Collins, P. H. (1989). The construction of Black feminist thought. *Signs, 14*(4), 745–773.

Collins, P. H. (1998). *Fighting words: Black women and the search for justice.* Minneapolis: University of Minnesota Press.

Collins, P. H. (1999). *Black feminist thought: Knowledge, consciousness, and the politics of empowerment.* New York: Routledge.

Collins, P. H. (2000). *Black feminist thought: Knowledge, consciousness, and the politics of empowerment* (2nd ed.). New York: Routledge.

Collins, P. H. (2003). Toward an Afrocentric feminist epistemology. In Y. S. Lincoln & N. K. Denzin (Eds.), *Turning points in qualitative research* (pp. 47–72). Walnut Creek, CA: Altamira Press.

Collins, P. H. (2010). The new politics of community. *American Sociological Review, 75*(1), 7–30.

Committee on Policy for Racial Justice. (1989). *Visions of a better way.* Washington, DC: Joint Center for Political Studies; Lanham, MD: University Press of America.

Connelly, F. M., & Clandinin, D. J. (1999). *Shaping a professional identity.* New York: Teachers College Press.

Cook, D. (1985). The history of hip hop. *Davey D's Hip Hop Corner.* Retrieved from www.daveyd.com/raptitle.html

Cook, D. A. (2010). Disrupted but not destroyed: Fictive-kinship networks among Black educators in post-Katrina New Orleans. *Southern Anthropologist, 35*(2), 1–25.

Cook, L., & Friend, M. (1991). Collaboration in special education: Coming of age in the 1990s. *Preventing School Failure, 35*(2), 24–27.

Cook, L., & Friend, M. (2010). The state of the art of collaboration on behalf of students with disabilities. *Journal of Educational & Psychological Consultation, 20*(1), 1–8.

Council of Graduate Schools. (2012). *Attrition and completion.* Retrieved from www. cgsnet.org/attrition-and-completion

Cozart, S. C. (2010). When the spirit shows up: An autoethnography of spiritual reconciliation with the academy. *Educational Studies, 46*(2), 250–269.

D'Amour, D., Ferrada-Videla, M., San Martin Rodriguez, L., & Beaulieu, M. D. (2005). The conceptual basis for interprofessional collaboration: Core concepts and theoretical frameworks. *Journal of Interprofessional Care, 19*(S1), 116–131.

Dantley, M. E. (2005). African American spirituality and Cornel West's notion of prophetic pragmatism: Restructuring educational leadership in American urban schools. *Educational Administration Quarterly, 41*(4), 651–674.

Davis, M., Dias-Bowie, Y., Greenberg, K., Klukken, G., Pollio, H. R., Thomas, S., & Thompson, C. L. (2004). "A fly in the buttermilk": Descriptions of university life by successful Black undergraduate students at a predominately white southeastern university. *Journal of Higher Education, 75.* Retrieved from http://trace.tennessee.edu/cgi/viewcontent.cgi?article=1074&context=utk_nurspubs

Davis, O. I. (2008). A visitation from the foremothers: Black women's healing through a 'performance of care'—from African Diaspora to the American academy. *Women's Studies in Communication, 31*(2), 175–185.

Denzin, N. (1997). *Interpretive ethnography—ethnographic practices for the 21st century.* Thousand Oaks, CA: Sage.

Denzin, N. K., & Lincoln, Y. S. (Eds.). (2005). *The Sage handbook of qualitative research.* Thousand Oaks, CA: Sage.

Dewey, J. (1938). *Experience and education.* New York: Kappa Delta Pi.

Dewey, J. (1997). *John Dewey: Experience and education.* New York: Touchstone.

Dewey, J. (2010). *How we think.* New York: FQ Books.

Dillard, C. B. (2006). *On spiritual strivings: Transforming an African American woman's academic life.* Albany: State University of New York Press.

Dimitriadis, G. (1996). Hip Hop: From live performance to mediated narrative. *Popular Music, 15*(2), 179–194.

Dixson, A. D., & Rousseau, C. K. (2005). And we are still not saved: Critical race theory in education ten years later. *Race, Ethnicity and Education, 8*(1), 7–27.

Dochy, F., Segers, M., & Buehl, M. M. (1999). The relation between assessment practices and outcomes of studies: The case of research on prior knowledge. *Review of Educational Research, 69,* 145–186.

Document and Designs. (2012). West African Adinkra symbols & translation. *Documents and Designs.* Retrieved from www.documentsanddesigns.com/reception_accessories/Cultural/African/Resourse_Adinkra_Symbols.htm

Dowdy, J. K. (2008). Fire and ice: The wisdom of Black women in the academy. *New Horizons in Adult Education and Human Resource Development, 22*(1), 24–43.

Du Bois, W. E. B. (1935). Does the Negro need separate schools? *Journal of Negro Education, 7,* 335.

Du Bois, W. E. B. (1903/1989). *The souls of Black folk.* New York: Bantam Books.

Duran, A. (n.d.). Creating successful partnerships with parents of first generation students. *Innovative Educators.* Retrieved from www.innovativeeducators.org/product_p/576.htm

Ebaugh, H. R., & Curry, M. (2000). Fictive kin as social capital in new immigrant communities. *Sociological Perspectives, 43*(2), 189–209.

Echevarría, J., Vogt, M., & Short, D. J. (2008). *Making content comprehensible for English learners: The SIOP model.* Boston, MA: Pearson, Allyn and Bacon.

Edwards, A. E. (2000). Community mothering: The relationship between mothering and the community work of Black women. *Journal of the Motherhood Initiative for Research and Community Involvement, 2*(2), 87–100.

Ehrhart-Morrison, D. (1997). *No mountain high enough: Secrets of successful African American women.* Berkeley, CA: Conari Press.

Ellis, C. (2004). *The ethnographic I: A methodological novel about autoethnography.* Walnut Creek, CA: Altamira Press.

Ellis, E. M. (2001). The impact of race and gender on graduate school socialization, satisfaction with doctoral study and commitment to degree completion. *Western Journal of Black Studies, 25*(1), 30–45.

Ellison, R. (1952/1995). *Invisible man.* New York: Vintage Books.

Erikson, E. (1956). The problem of ego identity. Journal of the American Psychoanalytic Association, 4, 56–121.

Erickson, F. (1987). Transformation and school success: The politics and culture of educational achievement. *Anthropology & Education Quarterly, 18*(4), 335–356.

Erikson, E. H. (1974). *Dimensions of a new identity.* New York: Norton.

Erikson, E. H., Paul, I. H., Heider, F., & Gardner, R. W., (1959). *Psychological issues.* New York: International Universities Press.

Faber, A. J., Willerton, E., Clymer, S. R., MacDermid, S. M., & Weiss, H. M. (2008). Ambiguous absence, ambiguous presence: A qualitative study of military reserve families in wartime. *Journal of Family Psychology, 22,* 222–230.

Fallon, M. V. (1997). The school counselor's role in first generation students' college plans. *School Counselor, 44*(5), 384–393.

Felder, P. (2010). On doctoral student development: Exploring faculty mentoring in the shaping of African American doctoral student success. *The Qualitative Report, 15*(2), 455–474.

Felder, P. P., & Baker, M. J. (2013). Extending Bell's Concept of Interest Convergence: A framework for understanding the African American doctoral student experience. *International Journal of Doctoral Studies, 8,* 1–21.

Fleischmann, C. M., Pagni, P. J., & Williamson, R. B. (1993). Exploratory back draft experiments. *Fire Technology, 29*(4), 298–316.

Fleming, J. (1984). *Blacks in college: A comparative study of students' success in Black and White institutions.* San Francisco, CA: Jossey-Bass.

Fletcher, E., Mel, G. M., & Robinson, B. (Composers). (1982). *The Message* [Album performed by Grandmaster Flash and the Furious Five]. New York: Sugar Hill Records.

Foner, N. (2001). West Indian migration to New York: An overview. In N. Foner (Ed.), *Islands in the city: West Indian migration to New York* (pp. 1–22). Berkeley: University of California Press.

Fordham, S. (1996). *Blacked out: Dilemmas of race, identity and success at Capitol High.* Chicago, IL: University of Chicago Press.

Fordon, A. E. (1996). Female doctoral students: An analysis of their lives and educational experiences through personal narratives (women doctoral students) (Doctoral Dissertation, University of Cincinnati, 1996). *Dissertation Abstracts International, 58*(01A), 104. (DAI No. AAI9718261).

Foster, M. (1993). Othermothers: Exploring the educational philosophy of Black American women teachers. In M. Arnot & K. Weiler (Eds.), *Feminism and social justice in education: International perspectives* (pp. 101–123). London: RoutledgeFalmer.

Freire, P. (1970). *Pedagogy of the oppressed.* New York: Continuum

Freire, P. (1992). *Pedagogy of the oppressed.* New York: Continuum.

Freire, P. (1994). *Pedagogy of hope: Reliving pedagogy of the oppressed* (R. R. Barr, trans.). New York: Continuum.

Freire, P. (2000). *Pedagogy of the oppressed.* (M. B. Ramos, trans., with introduction by D. Macedo). (30th anniversary ed.). New York: Continuum.

Freire, P. (2004). *Pedagogy of the oppressed*. New York: Continuum.

Friend, M., & Cook, L. (2013). *Interactions: Collaboration skills for school professionals* (7th ed.). Columbus, OH: Merrill/Pearson.

Fries-Britt, S., & Turner Kelly, B. (2005). Retaining each other: Narratives of two Africa American women in the academy. *The Urban Review, 37*(3), 221–242.

Fries-Britt, S., & Turner, B. (2002). Uneven stories: Successful Black collegians at a Black and White campus. *Review of Higher Education, 25*(3), 315–330.

Gajda, R. (2004). Utilizing collaborative theory to evaluate strategic alliances. *The American Journal of Evaluation, 25*(1), 65–77.

Gardner, S. K. (2009). The development of doctoral students: Phases of challenge and support. San Francisco, CA: Jossey-Bass.

Garvey, M. (1983). *The Marcus Garvey and Universal Negro Improvement Association Papers* (Vol. 7). R. A. Hill (Ed.). Oakland: University of California Press.

Gasman, M., Gerstl-Pepin, C., Anderson-Thompkins, S., Rasheed, L., & Hathaway, K. (2004). Developing trust, negotiating power: Transgressing race and status in the academy. *Teachers College Record, 106*(4): 689–715.

Gasman, M., Hirschfeld, A., & Vultaggio, J. (2008). "Difficult yet rewarding": The experiences of African American graduate students in education at an Ivy League institution. *Journal of Diversity in Higher Education, 1*(2), 126–138.

Gause, C. (2008). *Integration matters: Navigating identity, culture, and resistance*. New York: Peter Lang.

Gay, G. (2004). Navigating marginality en route to the professoriate: Graduate students of color learning and living in academia. *International Journal of Qualitative Studies in Education (QSE), 17*(2), 265–287. Retrieved from EBSCOhost.

Generett, G. G., & Cozart, S. (2012). The spirit bears witness: Reflections of two Black women's journey in the academy. *Negro Educational Review, 62–63*(1–4), 141–165.

George, N. (1992). *Buppies, B-Boys, Baps & BoHos: Notes on post-soul Black culture*. New York: HarperCollins.

Gibson, J. J. (1977). The theory of affordances. In R. E. Shaw & J. Bransford (Eds.), *Perceiving, acting, and knowing*. Hillsdale, NJ: Lawrence Erlbaum.

Gildersleeve, R. E., Croom, N. N., & Vasquez, P. L. (2011). "Am I going crazy?!": A critical race analysis of doctoral education. *Equity & Excellence in Education, 44*(1), 93–114.

Glenn, C. L. (2012). Stepping in and stepping and stepping out: Examining the way anticipatory career socialization impacts identity negation of African American Women in academia. In G. Gutiérez y Muhs, Y. Flores Newmann, C. G. Gonzalez, & A. P. Harris (Eds.), *Presumed incompetent: The intersections of race and class for women in academia* (pp. 133–141). Boulder: University Press of Colorado.

Glick, J. E., & Hohman-Marriott, B. (2007). Academic performance of young children in immigrant families: The significance of race, ethnicity, and national origins. *International Migration Review, 41*(2), 371–402.

Golde, C. M. (2000). Should I stay or should I go? Student descriptions of the doctoral attrition process. *The Review of Higher Education, 23,* 199–227.

Grason, S. (2005). *Journaloution: Journaling to awaken your inner voice, heal your life, and manifest your dreams.* Novato, CA: New World Library.

Green, A. M. (2008). A dream deferred: The experience of an African American student in a doctoral program in science. *Education, 128*(3), 339–348.

Green, C. E., & King, V. G. (2001). Sisters mentoring sisters: Africentric leadership development for Black women in the academy. *Journal of Negro Education, 70*(3), 156–165.

Greenleaf, R. K. (1982). *The servant as leader.* Westfield, IN: Robert K. Greenleaf Center.

Gregory, S. T. (1999). *Black women in the academy: The secrets to success and achievement.* Lanham, MD: University Press of America.

Griffin, K. A. (2013). Voices of the "othermothers": Reconsidering black professors' relationships with black students as a form of social exchange. *The Journal of Negro Education, 82*(2), 169–183.

Guiffrida, D. (2005). Othermothering as a framework for understanding African American students' definition of student-centered faculty. *Journal of Higher Education, 76*(6), 701–723.

Harris, A. P., & González, C. G. (2012). Introduction. In G. Gutiérez y Muhs, Y. Flores Newmann, C. G. Gonzalez, & A. P. Harris (Eds.), *Presumed incompetent: The intersections of race and class for women in academia* (pp. 1–14). Boulder: University Press of Colorado.

Harris, N. H. (1956). Desegregation in North Carolina. *The Journal of Negro Education, 25*(3), 299–306.

Hill, R. (1972). Strengths of Black Families. New York: National Urban League.

Hinton, D. (2010). Creating community on the margins: The successful Black female academician. *Urban Review, 42*(5), 394–402. doi:10.1007/s11256-009-0140-3

Hoge, C., Castro, C., & Eaton, K. (2006). *Impact of combat duty in Iraq and Afghanistan on family functioning: Findings from the Walter Reed Army Institute of Research Land Combat Study.* Human Factors and Medicine Panel Symposium (HFM-134) on Human Dimensions in Military Operations. Military Leaders' Strategies for Addressing Stress and Psychological Support.

Holland, D., Skinner, D., Lachiocotte, W., & Cain, C. (1998). *Identity and agency in cultural worlds.* Cambridge, MA: Harvard University Press.

Holmes, S. L., Land, L., & Hinton-Hudson, V. D. (2007). Race still matters: Considerations for mentoring Black women in academe. *Negro Educational Review, 58*(1/2), 105–129.

hooks, b. (1984). *Feminist theory: From margin to center.* Boston, MA: South End Press.

hooks, b. (1986). *Feminist theory: From margin to center.* Boston, MA: South End Press.

hooks, b. (1990). Postmodern Blackness. In b. hooks, *Yearning: Race, gender, and cultural politics* (pp. 23–31). Boston, MA: South End Press. Retrieved from www.maria buszek.com/kcai/PoMoSeminar/Readings/hooksPoMoBlckness.pdf hooks, b. (1993). *Sisters of the yam: Black women and self-recovery.* Boston, MA: South End Press.

hooks, b. (1994). *Teaching to transgress: Education as the practice of freedom.* New York: Routledge.

hooks, b. (2001). *Salvation: Black people and love.* New York: HarperCollins.

hooks, b. (2003). *Teaching community: A pedagogy of hope.* New York: Routledge.

Hord, F. L., & Lee, J. S. (Eds.). (1995). *I am because we are: Readings in Black philosophy.* Boston: University of Massachusetts Press.

Howard, A., & Levine, A. (2004). Where are the poor students? A conversation about social class and college attendance. *About Campus, 9*(4), 19–24.

Howard-Hamilton, M. F. (2003). Theoretical frameworks for African American women. *New Directions for Student Services, 2003,* 19–27.

Hubbell, K., & Burman, M. E. (2006). Factors related to successful collaboration in community campus partnerships. *The Journal of Nursing Education, 45*(12), 519–522.

Hunn, L. M. (2004). Africentric philosophy: A remedy for Eurocentric dominance. *New Directions for Adult and Continuing Education, 102,* 65–74.

Hurtado, A. (1996). Strategic suspensions: Feminists of color theorize the production of knowledge. In N. Goldberger, J. Tarule, B. Clinchy, & M. Belenky (Eds.), *Knowledge, difference, and power: Essays inspired by women's ways of knowing* (pp. 372–392). New York: Basic Books.

Huxham, C., & Vangen, S. (2000). Ambiguity, complexity and dynamics in the membership of collaboration. *Human Relations, 53*(6), 771–806.

Hyater-Adams, Y. A. (2010). Learning diversity and leadership skills through transformative narratives. *Tamara Journal for Critical Organization Inquiry, 8*(3/4), 208–232.

Jackson, C. H., Kite, M. E., & Branscombe, N. R. (1996). *African-American women's mentoring experiences.* Paper presented at the annual meeting of the American Psychological Association, Toronto, Ontario.

Jackson, L. R. (1998). The influence of both race and gender on the experiences of African American college women. *The Review of Higher Education, 21*(4), 359–375.

Jackson, S. (1999). Putting 'our inspiration to good use.' *Black Issues in Higher Education, 16,* 11–28.

Jackson, S. (2004). *Differently academic? Developing lifelong learning for women in higher education.* Norwell, MA: Kluwer Academic Publishers.

Jagers, J. J., & Smith, P. (1996). Further examination of the spirituality scale. *The Journal of Black Psychology, 22*(4), 429–442.

Jairam, D., & Kahl, D. H. (2012). Navigating the doctoral experience: The role of social support in successful degree completion. *International Journal of Doctoral Studies, 7,* 311–329.

James, S. M. (1993). Mothering: A possible Black feminist link to social transformation? In A. P. Busia, & S. M. James (Eds.), *Theorizing Black feminisms: The visionary pragmatism of Black women* (pp. 44–55). New York: Routledge.

Jolie, A. (2013, May 14). My medical choice. *New York Times* (The Opinion Pages). Retrieved from www.nytimes.com/2013/05/14/opinion/my-medical-choice.html/ ?_r=0

Jones, T. B., Wilder, J., & Osborne-Lampkin, L. (2013). Employing a black feminist approach to doctoral advising: Preparing black women for the professoriate. *The Journal of Negro Education, 82*(3), 326–338.

Karney, B., Loughran, D., & Pollard, M. (2012). Comparing marital status and divorce status in civilian and military populations. *Journal of Family Issues, 33,* 1572–1594. doi:10.1177/0192513X12439690

Kasinitz, P. (1992). *Caribbean New York.* Ithaca, NY: Cornell University Press.

Kasinitz, P. (2001). Invisible no more? West Indian Americans in the social scientific imagination. In N. Foner (Ed.), *Islands in the city: West Indian migration to New York* (pp. 257–275). Berkeley: University of California Press.

Keeling, R. P. (Ed.). (2004, January). *Learning reconsidered: A campus-wide focus on the student experience.* National Association of Student Personnel Administrators, American College Personnel Association. Retrieved from www.naspa.org/images/uploads/ main/Learning_Reconsidered_Report.pdf

Keller, U., & Tillman, K. H. (2008). Post-secondary educational attainment of immigrant and native youth. *Social Forces, 87*(1), 121–152.

Kent, M. M. (2007). Immigration and America's Black population. *Population Bulletin, 62*(4), 1–16.

Kilgore, D. (2004). Toward a postmodern pedagogy. *New Directions for Adult & Continuing Education, 102,* 45–53.

Kitwana, B. (2002). *The hip-hop generation: Young Blacks and the crisis in African-American culture.* New York: BasicCivitas.

Kolb, D. (1984). *Experiential learning: Experience as the source of learning and development.* Upper Saddle River, NJ: Prentice Hall.

Ladson-Billings, G. (2005). *Beyond the big house: African American educators on teacher education.* New York: Teachers College Press.

Lawrence-Lightfoot, S. (2005). A dialogue between art and science. *Qualitative Inquiry, 11*(1), 3–15.

Lee, R. (2014, May 24). *Home may be more stressful than at work, new research warns.* Retrieved from www.techtimes.com/articles/7461/20140524/home-may-be-more-stressful-than-at-work-new-research-warns.htm

Loder, T. L. (2005). African American women principals' reflections on social change, community othermothering, and Chicago Public School reform. *Urban Education, 40*(3), 298–320.

Loeb, P. R. (2004). *The impossible will take a little while: A citizen's guide to hope in a time of fear.* New York: Basic Books.

Lorde, A. (2007). *Sister outsider: Essays and speeches by Audre Lorde.* New York: Random House.

Lowe, K., Adams, K., Brown, B., & Hinkle, K. (2012). Impact of military deployment on family relationships. *Journal of Family Studies, 18*(1), 17–27.

Luft, J., & Ingham, H. (1955). *The Johari window, a graphic model of interpersonal awareness. Proceedings of the western training laboratory in group development.* Los Angeles: University of California Extension Office.

Mansfield, A. J., Kaufman, J. S., Marshall, S. W., Gaynes, B. N., Morrissey, J. P., & Engel, C. C. (2010). Deployment and the use of mental health services among U.S. Army wives. *New England Journal of Medicine, 362,* 101–109.

Martinez, J. A., Sher, K. J., Krull, J. L., & Wood, P. K. (2009). Blue-collar scholars?: Mediators and moderators of university attrition in first-generation college students. *Journal of College Student Development, 50*(1), 87–103.

Massey, D. S., Mooney, M., Torres, K. C., & Charles, C. Z. (2007). Black immigrants and Black natives attending selective colleges and universities in the United States. *American Journal of Education, 113,* 243–271.

Mattis, J. S. (2000). African American women's definition of spirituality and religiosity. *Journal of Black Psychology, 26*(1), 101–122.

Mattis, J. S., & Jagers, R. J. (2001). A relational framework for the study of religiosity and spirituality in the lives of African Americans. *Journal of Community Psychology, 29*(5), 519–539.

Mawhinney, L. (2012). Othermothering: A personal narrative exploring relationships between black female faculty and students. *Negro Educational Review, 62/63*(1–4), 213–232, 266.

McIntosh, P. (1990). White privilege: Unpacking the invisible knapsack. *Independent School, 49*(2), 31–35.

Merriam, S. B. (2002). *Qualitative research in practice: Examples for discussion and analysis.* San Francisco, CA: Jossey-Bass.

Merriweather Hunn, L. M. (2008). Proof in the pudding: Does Guiffrida's cultural advancement of Tinto's theory apply to African American graduate students? *Journal of Ethnographic & Qualitative Research, 2,* 255–263.

Miller Dyce, C. (2009). Social capital as village network: Rethinking the nature of parental involvement in the precollege preparation of African American students (Unpublished doctoral dissertation). University of North Carolina, Greensboro.

Mitchell, N. (2005). Academic achievement among Caribbean immigrant adolescents: The impact of generational status on academic self-concept. *Professional School Counseling, 8*(3), 209–218.

Montrosse, B. E., & Young, C. J. (2012). Market demand for special education faculty. *Teacher Education and Special Education: The Journal of the Teacher Education Division of the Council for Exceptional Children, 35*(2), 140–153.

Morgan, J. (1999). *When Chickenheads come home to roost: A hip-hop feminist breaks it down.* New York: Touchstone.

Moses, Y. T. (1989). *Black women in academe: Issues and strategies.* Washington, DC: Association of American Colleges.

Murata, A. (2006). Bridging identities: Making sense of who we are becoming to be. In T. R. Berry & N. Mizelle (Eds.), *From oppression to grace: Women of color and their dilemmas in the academy* (pp. 24–33). Sterling, VA: Stylus.

National Center for Educational Statistics. (2010). Table 303: Doctor's degrees conferred by degree-granting institutions, by sex, race/ethnicity, and field of study, 2008–2009. *Digest of Educational Statistics.* Retrieved from http://nces.ed.gov/programs/digest/d10/tables/dt10_303.asp

National Center for Education Statistics. (2012). Table 237: Total fall enrollment in degree-granting institutions, by level of student, sex, attendance status, and race/ethnicity, selected years, 1976-2010. *Digest of Education Statistics.* Retrieved from: http://nces.ed.gov/pubs2012/2012001.pdf

Nash, R. J. (2004). *Liberating scholarly writing: The power of personal narrative.* New York, NY: Teachers College Press.

Naumann, W. C., Bandalos, D., & Gutkin, T. B. (2003). Identifying variables that predict college success for first-generation college students. *The Journal of College Admission, 181*, 4–9.

Nerad, M., & Miller, D. S. (1997). The institution cares: Berkeley's efforts to support dissertation writing in the humanities and social sciences. *New Directions for Higher Education, 25*(3), 75–90.

Obama, B. (2008, August 28). Address accepting the presidential nomination at the Democratic National Convention in Denver: "The American Promise." Retrieved from The American Presidency Project website at www.presidency.ucsb.edu/ws/index.php?pid=78284

Ogbu, J. U. (2007). African American education: A cultural ecological perspective. In H. P. McAdoo (Ed.), *Black families* (pp. 79–94). Thousand Oaks, CA: Sage.

Ogbu, J. U., & Simons, H. D. (1998). Voluntary and involuntary minorities: A cultural-ecological theory of school performance with some implications for education. *Anthropology & Education Quarterly, 29*(2), 155–188.

Okpalaoka, C. L., & Dillard, C. B. (2011). Our healing is next to the wound: Endarkened feminisms, spirituality, and wisdom for teaching, learning and research. *New Directions for adult and continuing education, 131*, 65–73.

Oyserman, D., Harrison, K., & Bybee, D. (2001). Can racial identity be promotive of academic efficacy? *International Journal of Behavioral Development, 23*(4), 379–385.

Pajares, F., & Schunk, D. H. (2005). Self-efficacy and self-concept beliefs. In H. W. Marsh, R. G. Craven, & D. M. McInerney (Eds.), *International advances in self research: New frontiers for self-research* (Vol. 2, pp. 95–121). Greenwich, CT: Information Age.

Patterson, D. M. (2006). *Divorcing the doctor: Black women doctoral students and their intimate relationships during the doctoral process* (Unpublished doctoral dissertation). Washington State University, Pullman, PA.

Patton, L. (2009). My sister's keeper: A qualitative examination of mentoring experiences among African American women in graduate and professional schools. *The Journal of Higher Education, 80*(5), 510–537.

Patton, L. D., & Harper, S. R. (2003). Mentoring relationships among African American women in graduate and professional schools. *New Directions for Student Services*, 67–78.

Patton, T. (2004). Reflections of a Black woman professor: Racism and sexism in academia. *Howard Journal of Communications*, 15(3), 185–200. doi:101080/10646170490483629

Patton, L. D., & Harper, S. R. (2003). Mentoring relationships among African American women in graduate and professional schools. *New Directions for Student Services*, 2003(104), 67–78.

Paulus, B., & Nijstad, P. B. (Eds.). (2003). *Group creativity: Innovation through collaboration*. New York: Oxford University Press.

Phelps, R. E., Taylor, J. D., & Gerard, P. A. (2001). Cultural mistrust, ethnic identity, racial identity, and self-esteem among ethnically diverse Black university students. *Journal of Counseling & Development*, 79, 209–216.

Piaget, J. (1970). *Genetic epistemology*. New York: Columbia University Press.

Pierce, C. (1974). Psychiatric problems of the Black minority. In S. Arieti (Ed.), American handbook of psychiatry (pp. 515). New York: Basic Books.

Plato. (1992). *Republic* (G. M. A. Grube, trans.). Indianapolis, IN: Hackett.

Prakash, O. (2012). *From change to transformation and beyond: Maintaining balance on the fast track*. Bloomington, IN: iUniverse.

Pratt, M. L. (1991). Arts of the contact zone. *Profession*, 33–40. New York: MLA.

Pride, F. (2007). *The message: 100 life lessons from hip-hop's greatest songs*. Philadelphia, PA: Thunder's Mouth Press.

Reagon, B. J. (1983). Coalition politics: Turning the century. In B. Smith (Ed.), *Home girls: A Black feminist anthology* (pp. 356–368). New York: Kitchen Table Press.

Reay, D. (2000). A useful extension of Bourdieu's conceptual framework: Emotional capital as a way of understanding mothers' involvement in their children's education. *Sociological Review*, 48(4), 568–585.

Riehl, R. J. (1994). The academic preparation, aspirations, and first-year performance of first-generation students. *College and University*, 70, 14–19.

Roach, R. (2005). Drawing upon the diaspora. *Diverse: Issues in Higher Education*, 22(14), 38–41.

Robinson, C. (1999) Developing a mentoring program: A graduate student's reflection of change. *Peabody Journal of Education*, 74(2), 119–134.

Rodriguez, D. (2006). Un/masking identity: Healing our wounded souls. *Qualitative Inquiry*, 12(6), 1067–1090.

Rong, X. L., & Brown, F. (2002). Socialization, culture and identities of Black immigrant children: What educators need to know and do. *Education and Urban Society*, 34, 247–273.

Rose, J. F. (1990). Psychologic health of women: A phenomenologic study of women's inner strength. *Advances in Nursing Science*, 12(2), 1–84.

Rosenthal, C. J. (1985). Kinkeeping in the familial division of labor. *Journal of Marriage and the Family*, 47(4), 965-974.

Ruiz, D. M. (1997). *The four agreements: A practical guide to personal freedom*. San Rafael, CA: Amber-Allen.

Ryan, R. M., Stiller, J. D., & Lynch, J. H. (1994). Representations of relationships to teachers, parents, and friends as predictors of academic motivation and self-esteem. *The Journal of Early Adolescence, 14*(2), 226–249.

Sanders, M. G. (2012). African American families and education. In J. A. Banks (Ed.), *Encyclopedia of Diversity in Education, 1*, 40–41.

Schallert, D. L. (1982). The significance of knowledge: A synthesis of research related to schema theory. In W. Otto & S. White (Eds.), *Reading expository prose* (pp. 13–18). New York: Academic.

Schwarzenegger, A. (n.d.). BrainyQuote.com. Retrieved from www.brainyquote.com/quotes/quotes/a/arnoldschw116694.html

Scott, G. A. (2013). Individuals with Disabilities Education Act: Standards needed to improve identification of racial and ethnic overrepresentation in special education: GAO-13-137. U.S. Government Office of Accountability. Retrieved from www.gao.gov/assets/660/653446.txt

Shapiro, S. (2006). *Losing heart: The moral and spiritual mis-education of America's children*. Mahwah, NJ: Lawrence Erlbaum.

Simmonds, F. N. (1992). Difference, power, and knowledge: Black women in academia. In H. Hinds, A. Phoenix, & J. Stacey (Eds.), *Working out: New directions for women's studies* (pp. 51–60). Bristol, PA: Falmer Press.

Smith, J. K. (1997). The stories educational researchers tell about themselves. *Educational Researcher, 26*(5), 4–11.

Smith, M. J. (2008). College choice process of first-generation Black female students: Encouraged to what end? *Negro Educational Review, 59*(3–4), 147.

Solórzano, D., Ceja, M., & Yosso, T. (2000). Critical race theory, racial microaggressions, and campus racial climate: The experiences of African American college students. *Journal of Negro Education, 69*(1/2), 60–73.

Springer, K. (1999). *Still lifting, still climbing: African American women's contemporary activism*. New York: NYU Press.

Steele, C. M. (1997). A threat in the air: How stereotypes shape intellectual identity and performance. *American Psychologist, 52*(6), 613–629.

Steele, C. M., & Aronson, J. (1995). Stereotype threat and the intellectual test performance of African-Americans. *Journal of Personality and Social Psychology, 69*, 797–811.

Steiner, R. (1923). Education and healing. Lecture at the Waldorf School. Retrieved from www.waldorflibrary.org/rudolf-steiner-resources/articles-by-rudolf-steiner/627-education-and-healing

Stevens, K. C. (1980). The effect of background knowledge on the reading comprehension of ninth graders. *Journal of Reading Behavior, 12*(2), 151–154.

Stewart III, C. F., (1999). Black Spirituality and Black Consciousness, Africa World Press, Inc., Trenton, NJ.

Stohs, J. H. (2000). Multicultural women's experience of household labor, conflicts, and equity. *Sex Roles, 42*(5/6), 339–361.

Stone, M. D. (2000, January). Talking with dinosaurs. *Adults Learning, 11*(5), 26.

Strangman, N., Hall, T., & Meyer, A. (2004). Background knowledge instruction and the implications for UDL implementation. Retrieved from www.cast.org/publications/ncac/ncac_backknowledgeudl.html

Student, G. (2012). The other father. *Torah Musings.* Retrieved from www.torahmusings.com/2012/05/the-other-father/

Sue, D. W. (2010). *Microaggressions in everyday life: Race, gender, and sexual orientation.* Hoboken, NJ: John Wiley & Sons.

Swigonski, M. (1996, May). Challenging privilege through Afrocentric social work practice. *Social Work, 4*(1), 153–161.

Tafari, D. N. (2013, May). *Hip-hop is more than just music to me: A narrative study exploring the counter-stories of Black men elementary school teachers* (Unpublished Dissertation). University of North Carolina, Greensboro.

Tatum, B. D. (1997). *Why are all the Black kids sitting together in the cafeteria? And other conversations about race.* New York: Basic Books.

Taylor, R. J. (1988). Structural determinants of religious participation among Black Americans. *Review of Religious Research, 30*(2), 114–125.

Taylor, E., & Anthony, J. S. (2000). Stereotype threat reduction and wise schooling: Towards the successful socialization of African American doctoral students in education. *The Journal of Negro Education, 69*(3), 184–198.

Terenzini, P. T., Pascarella, E. T., & Blimling, G. S. (1996). Students' out of classroom experiences and their influence on learning and cognitive development: A literature review. *Journal of College Student Development, 37*(2), 149–162.

Thomas, G. D., & Hollenshead, C. (2001, Summer). Resisting from the margins: The coping strategies of Black women and other women of color faculty members at a research university. *Journal of Negro Education, 70*(3), 166–175.

Thompson, G. L. (1999). What the numbers really mean: African-American underrepresentation at the doctoral level. *Journal of College Student Retention, 1*(1), 23–40.

Thuesen, S. C. (2006). Pearsall Plan. In W. S. Powell (Ed.), *Encyclopedia of North Carolina* (p. 873). Chapel Hill: University of North Carolina Press.

Tinto, V., Russo, P., & Stephanie, K. (1994). Constructing educational communities: Increase retention in challenging circumstances. *Community College Journal, 64*(4), 18–22.

Trotman, F. K. (2009). The imposter phenomenon among African American women in U.S. institutions of higher education: Implications for counseling. *Compelling Counseling Interventions: VISTAS,* 77–87.

Truth, S. (1851). Ain't I a woman? Speech delivered at the Women's Convention, Akron, OH. Retrieved from www.feminist.com/resources/artspeech/genwom/sojour.htm

Vickerman, M. (2001). Tweaking a monolith: The West Indian immigrant encounter with "Blackness." In N. Foner (Ed.), *Islands in the city: West Indian migration to New York* (pp. 237–256). Berkeley: University of California Press.

Vickerman, M. (2007). Recent immigration and race: Continuity and change. *Du Bois Review, 4*(1), 141–165.

Viernes Turner, C. S. (2002). Women of color in academe: Living with multiple marginality. *The Journal of Higher Education, 73*(1), 74–93.

Villegas, A. M., & Lucas, T. (2007). The culturally responsive teacher. *Educational Leadership, 64*(6), 28–33.

Vogt, M. E. (2005). Improving achievement for ELLs through sheltered instruction. *Language Learner, 1*(1), 22, 25.

Wallerstein, J. S., & Kelly, J. B. (1981). *Surviving the breakup: How children and parents cope with divorce.* New York: Basic Books.

Washburn-Moses, L. (2007). Minority students' perceptions of their doctoral programs in special education. *Journal of Teacher Education, 58,* 456–469.

Watt, S. K. (2003). Come to the river: Using spirituality to cope, resist and develop identity. *New Directions for Student Services, 104,* 29–40.

Weisser, C. (2002). *Moving beyond academic discourse: Composition studies and the public sphere.* Carbondale: Southern Illinois University Press.

Williams, M. A. (2004). "I got mine, now you get yours": Derailing the underground railroad. In D. Cleveland (Ed.), *A long way to go: Conversations about race by African American faculty and graduate students* (p. 241). New York: Peter Lang.

Williamson, M. (1992). *A return to love: Reflections on the principles of a course in miracles.* New York: Harper Collins.

Woods, R. L. (2001). Invisible women: The experiences of Black female doctoral students at the University of Michigan. In A. L. Green & R. Mabokela (Eds.), *Sisters of the Academy: Emergent Black women scholars in higher education* (pp. 105–116). Sterling, VA: Stylus.

Contributors

Cheryll Sibley-Albold earned her PhD degree from the University of North Carolina at Greensboro. Her research areas of interest are social and professional identity development as well as academic self-efficacy and academic self-concept, particularly as they relate to academic performance, socialization, retention, and persistence.

Temeka L. Carter earned a PhD in Rhetoric and Composition at the University of North Carolina at Greensboro. Her academic interests include African American Studies, prophetic pragmatism, service-learning, feminism, and media studies.

Marrissa Dick earned a PhD in Educational Leadership and Cultural Foundations with a Specialization in Cultural Studies and a minor in Communication Studies at the University of North Carolina at Greensboro. Dr. Dick's academic interest includes Mis-Educative and Micro-Aggressive Experiences in the American educational system.

Cherrel Miller Dyce is an assistant professor of education and Faculty Fellow at The Center for Race, Ethnicity and Diversity Education at Elon University, Elon, North Carolina. Her research agenda includes issues related to diversity studies, educational inequities, precollege preparation of students of color, family and community involvement in education, student development, counseling, and mentoring.

Kim Pemberton, is currently the co-coordinator of Elementary Education at Winston Salem State University in Winston Salem, North Carolina. She earned a BS degree in Early Childhood Education from Winston-Salem State University, an MS degree in Elementary Education from North Carolina Agricultural & Technical State University, and her PhD from the University of North Carolina at Greensboro in Teacher Education. She also holds

Birth–Kindergarten certification and is Nationally Board Certified (Early Generalist).

Torry Reynolds is a higher education professional who is dedicated to the personal and academic success of college students. Her research interests include academic support programs, developmental education, and student advocacy.

Cynthia Shamberger, is an assistant professor in the department of Middle Grades, Secondary, and Specialized Subjects at Fayetteville State University, in Fayetteville, North Carolina. Her expertise includes inclusive school practices, collaboration among school professionals, co-teaching, and instructional strategies for students who struggle in math, reading, and writing.

Dawn Nicole Hicks Tafari is passionate about the arts, culture, education, and translating theory into practice. Her research interests include Black boys in public schools, Black male elementary school teachers, Hip-Hop culture's influence on identity development, Hip-Hop feminism, critical pedagogy, critical race theory, and narrative research.

LaWanda M. Wallace, is a professor in the Human Development & Service Department at North Carolina A&T State University. Her research interests include colorism, critical race theory, black feminist theory and issues dealing with social justice and advocacy.

Toni Milton Williams currently serves as an assistant professor in the Middle Level and Language & Literacy programs in the department of Instruction and Teacher Education at the University of South Carolina. Her research agenda includes life histories and identities of pre-service teachers, culturally responsive teaching and issues of social justice, critical literacy through a critical race lens.

Cynthia Brooks Wooten earned her PhD from the University North Carolina at Greensboro in Teacher Education with a concentration in Literacy. Her academic passion and commitment to the preparation of future teachers is epitomized in her work and appetite for lifelong learning.

ROCHELLE BROCK &
RICHARD GREGGORY JOHNSON III,
Executive Editors

Black Studies and Critical Thinking is an interdisciplinary series which examines the intellectual traditions of and cultural contributions made by people of African descent throughout the world. Whether it is in literature, art, music, science, or academics, these contributions are vast and far-reaching. As we work to stretch the boundaries of knowledge and understanding of issues critical to the Black experience, this series offers a unique opportunity to study the social, economic, and political forces that have shaped the historic experience of Black America, and that continue to determine our future. Black Studies and Critical Thinking is positioned at the forefront of research on the Black experience, and is the source for dynamic, innovative, and creative exploration of the most vital issues facing African Americans. The series invites contributions from all disciplines but is specially suited for cultural studies, anthropology, history, sociology, literature, art, and music.

Subjects of interest include (but are not limited to):

- EDUCATION
- SOCIOLOGY
- HISTORY
- MEDIA/COMMUNICATION
- RELIGION/THEOLOGY
- WOMEN'S STUDIES

- POLICY STUDIES
- ADVERTISING
- AFRICAN AMERICAN STUDIES
- POLITICAL SCIENCE
- LGBT STUDIES

For additional information about this series or for the submission of manuscripts, please contact Dr. Brock (Indiana University Northwest) at brock2@iun.edu or Dr. Johnson (University of San Francisco) at rgjohnsoniii@usfca.edu.

To order other books in this series, please contact our Customer Service Department:

(800) 770-LANG (within the U.S.)
(212) 647-7706 (outside the U.S.)
(212) 647-7707 FAX

Or browse online by series at www.peterlang.com.

Lightning Source UK Ltd.
Milton Keynes UK
UKHW020652170223
417189UK00016B/621